Sinclair Lewis

HOME AT LAST

Sinclair Lewis

HOME AT LAST

by John J. Koblas

VOYAGEUR PRESS

ISBN 0-89658-024-5

VOYAGEUR PRESS
9337 Nesbitt Rd.
Bloomington, MN 55437

For Isabel Lewis Agrell

Contents

	Acknowledgments	ix
	Sinclair Lewis: A Chronology	xi
	Foreword	xv
1	Sauk Centre	1
2	St. Cloud	26
3	St. Paul	37
4	Cass Lake	47
5	Minneapolis	53
6	Mankato	69
7	Elysian-Waterville	83
8	Saskatchewan	89
9	Pequot Lakes	98
10	Rainy Lake	104
11	Madison	106
12	Excelsior	114
13	Gunflint Trail	120
14	Duluth	123
	Reference Notes	143

Acknowledgments

THIS BOOK NEVER would have been written were it not for Isabel Lewis Agrell and Virginia Lewis, who so graciously permitted me to examine and use unpublished letters, diaries, photographs, and personal belongings of Claude and Sinclair Lewis. I am also indebted to Jean Archibald, librarian at the Weyerhaeuser Library at Macalester College in St. Paul, for permitting me to quote from letters of Sinclair Lewis that are part of a special collection.

I am deeply grateful to the following persons and the organizations they represent: Donald Gallup, curator, Beinecke Rare Book and Manuscript Library, New Haven, Connecticut; Marcia T. Schuster, director, Blue Earth County Historical Society, Mankato, Minnesota; David Gravdahl, James Harmon, and Lori Torbinson, Breezy Point Lodge, Pequot Lakes, Minnesota; Stanley Johnson, director, Cass County Historical Society, Cass Lake, Minnesota; Grant Utley, editor, *Cass Lake Times*; Sister Paul Mary of Holy Rosary Convent, Duluth, Minnesota; Willis Miller, publisher, *Hudson Star-Observer*, Hudson, Wisconsin; Mary Hilke, director, Koochiching County Historical Society, International Falls, Minnesota; Arlene Schwartz and James Hruska of the Le Sueur County Historical Society, Elysian, Minnesota; Dianne Goldstaub and Ken Berg of the *Mankato Free Press*; Robert Aden and Donald Stolz of the Old Log Theater, Excelsior, Minnesota; Tony Schulzetenberg, professor, St. Cloud State University, Center for Library and Audiovisual Education, St. Cloud, Minnesota; Mrs. Hugh F. Gwin, director, St. Croix County Historical Society, Hudson; and Kent Fuhrman, director, Sinclair Lewis Interpretive Center, Sauk Centre, Minnesota.

I am indebted to the following persons for sharing memories or assisting with vital research: Mary Agrell, Robert Agrell, Betty Alexander, Mr. and Mrs. Richard Anderson, Elsa Anneke, Dr. Stuart Lane Arey, Margaret Culkin Banning, Ellsworth Barnard, Mrs. George Bohannon, Eddie C. Bolte, Charles F. Brigham, Jr., Mr. and

Mrs. Charles Butler, Eric Carlson, Clayton Carpenter, F. G. Cassidy, Daniel Christensen, Alfred Clague, Dr. Harry Clark, Ida Compton, Mrs. Robert Congdon, Edna Coolidge, Mrs. John Dalrymple, Edward Day, Mrs. Adolph Dehn, Robert B. Doremus, Ben DuBois, Pat DuBois, Mrs. George Eldridge, James Ellwood, Mary Van Evera, R. Alain Everts, Mrs. Fred Francis, Robert L. Gale, Dan Gapen, Richard D. Gapen, Leonard Garaghty, Phillip Garaghty, Mrs. Cecil Girvin, Evelyn Glendenning, Nils Grossman, Constance Gunnufson, Mr. and Mrs. Robert Hamilton, Clark B. Hansen, Clement Haulpers, Virginia Haynes, Mrs. Joseph Herman, the late Mrs. Jared How, Virginia Hyvarinen, Donald Ice, Gunnar Johansen, Lucile Kane, Mr. and Mrs. Ralph Keller, E. L. Kells, Edward F. Kermott, Arthur King, Harriet P. Kipp, J. Harold Kittleson, Grace Knowlton, Barbara Landfield, Bruce Landfield, Meridel LeSueur, Hjalmar O. Lokensgard, Sharon K. Long, Paul Lunden, Frederick Manfred, Sandra Mason, Mrs. Charles McCadden, William McCadden, Wayne J. Merbach, Fern Michaels, Mr. and Mrs. Rudolph Miller, Alice Modrow, Jerry Parson, Mrs. Henry Paull, Mrs. Henry Pochman, Joseph Pohlman family, Mary Pohlman, Ricardo Quintana, Mr. and Mrs. Robert Ridder, Samuel Rogers, Mrs. Ralph Rosenberger, Russell Roth, Mrs. Norman Sandquist, Harold Schoelkopf, Chris Sherman, Carol Simonson, Glanville Smith, Kenneth Smith, Mrs. Cecil Snow, Mrs. Richard Spicer, Harold E. Stassen, Lois Swain, Ruth Swain, Edward Swanson, David G. Taylor, Carole Toman, Brenda Ueland, Kent Van Hoe, Donald Wandrei, Margaret Waterman, Mrs. Reginald Eyre Watters, Viola Wendt, Emma Wiecking, Eleanor Wirig, and Joseph Wise.

Words cannot express my gratitude to R. Dixon Smith, who read this book in manuscript and rescued me from a host of blunders.

I owe much more than a word of thanks to my wife, Lynette, my three daughters, Stacy, Stephanie, and Sarah, and my son, John, for putting up with my neglect, eccentricities, and typewriter ribbons these past two years.

John J. Koblas
Minneapolis, Minnesota
December 13, 1980

Sinclair Lewis: A Chronology

1885	Born in Sauk Centre, Minnesota.
1891	Death of mother, Emma Kermott Lewis.
1892	Father's marriage to Isabel Warner.
1902	First published work appeared in the *Sauk Centre Herald*.
1902–3	Entered Oberlin Academy, Oberlin, Ohio.
1903	Entered Yale University.
1904	Portland, Maine, and cattleboat trip to Liverpool, England.
1906	Second cattleboat trip.
	Upton Sinclair's Helicon Hall in Englewood, New Jersey.
	New York City.
	Panama.
1908	Graduation from Yale.
	Death of friend Arthur Upson.
1908–10	Journalistic experience: Waterloo, Iowa; New York; California; Washington.
1910–15	Employed by publishers in New York.
1912	Publication of *Hike and the Aeroplane*.
1914	Publication of *Our Mr. Wrenn*.
	Marriage to Grace Hegger.
1914–15	Port Washington, Long Island.
1915	Publication of *The Trail of the Hawk*.
1916	Sauk Centre to write *The Job*.
1917	Publication of *The Innocents*.
	Publication of *The Job*.
	New York City.
	Birth of first son, Wells.
1917–18	St. Paul.
	Cass Lake.
	Play *Hobohemia* presented.
1918–19	Minneapolis.
1919	Mankato.

	Publication of *Free Air*.
1920	Washington, D.C.
	Publication of *Main Street*.
1921	Death of stepmother, Isabel Warner Lewis.
1921–22	Hartford, Connecticut.
1922	Publication of *Babbitt*.
1923	Caribbean.
1923–25	Europe.
1924	Saskatchewan Indian treaty trip with his brother Claude.
1925	Publication of *Arrowsmith*.
	Washington, D.C.
1926	Pequot Lakes to work on *Elmer Gantry*.
	Rainy Lake.
	Death of father, E. J. Lewis.
	Declined Pulitzer Prize for *Arrowsmith*.
	Publication of *Mantrap*.
1927	Separation from Grace Hegger.
	Publication of *Elmer Gantry*.
	Europe.
1928	Europe.
	Divorce from Grace Hegger.
	Marriage to Dorothy Thompson.
	Publication of *The Man Who Knew Coolidge*.
	Twin Farms, Barnard, Vermont (summers through 1937).
1928–32	Winters in New York City.
1929	Publication of *Dodsworth*.
1930	Birth of second son, Michael.
	Nobel Prize.
1932–33	Europe.
1933	Publication of *Ann Vickers*.
1933–37	Winters in Bronxville, New York.
1934	Publication of *Work of Art*.
1935	Publication of *It Can't Happen Here*.
1936	Europe
	Received honorary degree from Yale.
1937	Bermuda.
	Separation from Dorothy Thompson.
1938	Publication of *The Prodigal Parents*.
1938–39	On tour with *Angela Is Twenty-Two*.
1940	Publication of *Bethel Merriday*.
	Teaches at the University of Wisconsin in Madison.

Visits Hemingway.
Cuba.

1941   New York.
Moves to Lakeville, Connecticut.

1942   Divorce from Dorothy Thompson.
Excelsior, Minnesota.
Teaches at the University of Minnesota in Minneapolis.

1943–46 Winters in New York City.

1943   Publication of *Gideon Planish*.

1944   Death of son Wells.

1944–46 Duluth.

1945   Publication of *Cass Timberlane*.

1946   Death of brother Fred.

1946–49 Thorvale Farm, South Williamstown, Massachusetts.

1947   Publication of *Kingsblood Royal*.
St. Paul, researching *The God-Seeker*.

1948–49 Italy.

1949   Publication of *The God-Seeker*.
Europe.

1949–51 Europe.

1951   Death in Rome.
Publication of *World So Wide*.

Foreword

THROUGHOUT A LIFE characterized by endless searching, Sinclair Lewis struggled to turn his back on the Midwest of his boyhood and dance to the rhythms of a different drum. Somehow he always returned to his native soil. In many of his books, he wrote about the Midwest, describing life in small towns and bustling cities, portraying real people who had played a role in the building of a community or who had eked out a meager existence. In *The God-Seeker* he chronicled the daring adventures of the Minnesota pioneer; in *Babbitt*, the gauche efforts of the average businessman attempting to thrust his greedy fingers ever deeper into the American pie; and in epics like *Free Air* and *Main Street*, the travesty that small-town America had become.

Physically and, undoubtedly, spiritually, he tried to come home when he wasn't lost in a whirlwind of travel. In a letter to niece Virginia Lewis dated November 12, 1937, he described his self-exile and apologized for their conflicting schedules:

> I am awfully sorry that I missed you in New York, and I was delighted that I had the chance to see your father even for a few minutes. I have just been in the West lecturing. The nearest I got to Minneapolis was Milwaukee and Cedar Rapids, Iowa. I go out again in January, but I don't believe that even then I shall be anywhere near you. Otherwise I had hoped that we would have a meal together.

Lewis, frequently called Harry or Hal but seldom by his middle name, Sinclair, liked to create the impression that he was happy in his wanderlust, but those who knew him best were able to see through the façade. He enjoyed giving advice regarding travel—how to move about inexpensively, where to stay, what to eat, and what to avoid at all costs. He seldom complained about missing trains, trams, and steamers but was more apt to bemoan the arduous task of staying home, as in a letter to Virginia Lewis dated December 29, 1943:

> I finished up my lecture tour all right—fairly hard going, 24 cities from Seattle to Houston and San Antonio to Eau Claire and Toronto, but we didn't miss a single date, though a good share of the trains were late. Then I came home and promptly came down with the flu—not at all serious, just coughing and a running nose and an indisposition to do anything so wildly difficult and enterprising as brush my teeth.

Able to jest over any experience, he concluded the description of his flu on a happy note:

> But it has given me a beautiful rest, after a couple of years of constant going, and I've been placidly—between sneezes— reading Dickens.

His attempts to cease such globe-trotting and follow his heart home were linked to his desire to write a major novel on his home ground. In 1916, with his first wife, Grace Hegger, he came home to Sauk Centre to write his fourth novel, *The Job*. He came home to St. Paul during the winter of 1917–18 to rewrite his play *Hobohemia* and again in 1947 to research and write his novel *The God-Seeker*. In 1918–19 he was back in Minneapolis to plot *Free Air* and *Main Street* and again in 1942 to write *Gideon Planish*. In 1919 he composed both *Free Air* and *Main Street* in Mankato. In 1924 he traversed the wilderness of Manitoba and Saskatchewan, an experience that would evolve into the novel *Mantrap*. In 1926 Pequot Lakes and Rainy Lake gave substance to *Elmer Gantry*. In 1940 he took refuge in Madison, Wisconsin, just 260 miles from Minneapolis, to prepare his play *Felicia Speaking* for Broadway. In 1942 he experienced life on Minnesota's Gunflint Trail and emerged with a short story, "All Wives Are Angels." From 1944 to 1946 he settled in Duluth and wrote two novels, *Cass Timberlane* and *Kingsblood Royal*.

He faced his most difficult confrontation in coming home to Sauk Centre after the publication of *Main Street* in 1920. He had offended nearly everyone in town by portraying them in his novel, and Carol Kennicott's thirty-two-minute stroll through downtown Gopher Prairie took in everybody and every business: Dyer's Drugstore; W. P. Kennicott, Physician and Surgeon; the Rosebud Movie Palace; Howland and Gould's Grocery; Dahl and Olson's Meat Market; a jewelry shop; a fly-buzzing saloon; the Smoke House tobacco shop; a clothing store; Haydock and Simon's Bon Ton Store; Axel Egge's General

Store; Sam Clark's Hardware Store; Chester Dashaway's House Furnishing Emporium; Billy's Lunch; a sour-smelling warehouse; a feed store; Ye Art Shoppe; Del Snafflin's Barber Shop and Pool Room; Nat Hicks' Tailor Shop; the Catholic church; the post office; the damp, yellow-brick schoolhouse; and the Farmer's National Bank.

In Gopher Prairie, Carol attended the meetings of the Jolly Seventeen Club, the Thanatopsis organization, the bridge parties, and the picnics—a round of life she found intolerably stifling. Canvassing the entire town, she found pleasure in only one building; not a dozen buildings suggested that in the fifty years of Gopher Prairie's existence anyone had realized that it was either desirable or possible to make this, one's own home, amusing or attractive.

Certainly Gopher Prairie is Lewis's hometown, Sauk Centre, but it is also a composite of Melrose, St. Cloud, Mankato, Rochester, Fergus Falls, Alexandria, Osakis, Faribault, and Taylors Falls—other Minnesota towns he had visited. In condemning the citizens of his hometown, he offended the citizens in every small town across the country.

The Sauk Centre he attacked in his portrayal of a "dull ugly Gopher Prairie," was, in 1920, a town of just under three thousand that grew by an average twenty-two people yearly and whose citizens feared urban sprawl and called their town the Butter Capital of the World.[1]

Today Sauk Centre has forgiven Lewis, as evidenced by the Sinclair Lewis Interpretive Center, the Sinclair Lewis Boyhood Home Museum, Sinclair Lewis Avenue, the "original" Main Street, the Main Street Cafe, Main Street Chevrolet, the Main Street Theater, and the high school athletic teams, which have adopted the name the Main Streeters. Almost everyone who makes a pilgrimage to the town for the first time reads *Main Street*.

Before Lewis wrote, many American authors followed the example of Henry James and others who borrowed exclusively from their English heritage.[2] Lewis became one of the leaders of a revival of naturalism and American Realism, urging other writers to shun Europe and look "back to America."

Lewis urged his fellow writers not to fall prey to the follies of their English brothers, who wrote about the glitter and false fronts of life; he urged Americans to present the America characterized by the average worker, engrossed in the drudgery of an eight-to-five job, who raises a family and ekes out an existence. He felt that enough had been written about shining knights and wand-toting fairy princesses; he aimed to place the common man, the real American, in proper perspective.

An entire school of authors embraced the same movement—giants like Theodore Dreiser, Sherwood Anderson, Vachel Lindsay, Edgar Lee Masters, Zona Gale, Thomas Wolfe, and, to a lesser degree, F. Scott Fitzgerald and Ernest Hemingway. But Lewis's *Main Street* served as the movement's catalyst.

The "back to America" crusade was not limited to the world of literature; there was a parallel movement in art. After experiencing the grim horrors of World War I, Americans were not ready to forget their pain and suffering, and they longed to see their emotions on canvas.[3]

The Ash Can School, founded by George Bellows, flourished in the 1920s and 1930s while pontifical critics in New York and London thumbed their noses at the honest, matter-of-fact realism, and the kings of wealth and princes of business sneered. The work of Bellows, whose lithographs portrayed New York tenements, backyards, deserted streets, dimly lit corners, and grim scenes from the Bowery, awakened a nation to the very real horrors of life in the big city.

There were others besides Bellows who engineered this movement. Arthur Dove and his School of Stylist Realism hung out America's dirty laundry for the world to see; Alfred Stieglitz, who photographed "realism," put his camera to work in the crusade; Georgia O'Keefe, a pioneer in the School of American Realism, painted shocking scenes such as a desert sand dune bearing a buffalo skull; and John Sloane revealed the backyards of America and the seaminess of street life.

It was the adolescence of a nation that made the American Realism movement popular. The new post-war generation exhibited different values than those embraced by its parents, and it longed to be part of a movement that it could call its own. The movement was so successful that funds were allocated to American art and design under the Works Progress Administration in 1935.

One of the reasons American Realism was successful was because the artists and writers borrowed from their own experience. Sinclair Lewis used his prairie boyhood in Sauk Centre to conjure up Gopher Prairie as it looked through the eyes of his protagonist, Carol Kennicott. He used his experiences so successfully that he caused a national controversy.

Lewis borrowed not only from Sauk Centre but from Minneapolis as well. With an eye on Minneapolis and its fashionable Lowry Hill district, he formed Cornucopia and Agency Hill, which served as the settings for such short stories as "All Wives Are Angels," "Nobody to Write About," and "Green Eyes: A Handbook of Jealousy."[4]

Minneapolis had left many impressions on the young author since his early visits to the city around the turn of the century and during his initial residency in the city during the winter of 1918–19. He was overwhelmed by the extravagant dwellings of the miller and lumber potentates who basked amid a cluster of garden-circled lakes. He was humbled by the small, eccentric bungalows with pergolas and pebble-dash brick. Lewis's explorations took him to charming apartment houses that were anything but similar to the tall, bleak monstrosities of the East. His travels took him as well to the railroad tracks, where he witnessed the poverty of decrepit shanties.

Many Midwest citizens contended that their cities served as the Zenith portrayed in *Babbitt*, but residents of Minneapolis and St. Paul had as valid a claim as any. Zenith is located in the fictional state of Winnemac. Both Winnemac and Minnesota are Indian names. Furthermore, a parallel can be drawn between *Winne-* and *Minne-*, and Lewis's description of Zenith in the opening pages of *Babbitt* is not entirely alien to the Twin Cities. Lewis writes of "shingle-tortured mansard" roofs, which were quite popular in Minnesota during the writing of the novel. The double-sloping roofs, Italian in origin, were introduced to Minnesota in the nineteenth century.

Lewis invented a host of small towns for his fiction, with names like Schoenstrom, New Kotka, Curlew, Plato, Vernon, St. Sebastian, Northernapolis, Scandia Crossing, Joralemon, Wakamin, and Grand Republic. The towns are distinctly Minnesotan in character, and their names have the ring of authentic Minnesota hamlets.

In the second chapter of his novel *Free Air*, Lewis's heroine is hopelessly mired in mud some sixty miles beyond Minneapolis between the burgs of Gopher Prairie and Schoenstrom. Milt Daggett, a Schoenstrom garage mechanic, comes to her rescue.

Lewis's town of Joralemon is used in several stories, including the novel *The Trail of the Hawk*. It is the home of young Carl "Hawk" Ericson, who becomes a famous stunt and exhibition flyer, and the first twelve chapters of the book are set in the Joralemon-Plato area. (Joralemon receives mention in several Lewis short stories, including "The Kidnapped Memorial.")

"Harri," a 1935 short story that resembles *Main Street*, is set in New Kotka in Otter Tail County, and Lewis is so precise as to specify that it is only a half-hour's drive from Fergus Falls. Lewis takes the opportunity to praise the Leaf Mountains and Inspiration Peak, a scenic area that had long been a favorite of his.

The town of Vernon appears in several short stories, including "The Willow Walk," "The Cat of the Stars," "Habeas Corpus,"

"Things," "A Matter of Business," and "The Shadowy Glass." A fusion of Minneapolis and St. Paul may have served as the fictional Vernon.

Northernapolis is the scene of "Joy-Joy," "The Ghost Patrol," and *Hobohemia*, the play Lewis wrote in St. Paul. Despite the *-apolis*, the city bears no resemblance to Minneapolis; Duluth probably served as its archetype.

Lewis uses a Grand Republic setting in two novels, *Cass Timberlane* and *Kingsblood Royal*. The city lies some eighty miles north of Minneapolis and seventy-odd miles from Duluth. Grand Republic is in reality the tiny hamlet of Arthyde superimposed onto Duluth. Grand Republic even has elegant residential neighborhoods such as Ottawa Heights and Sylvan Park. Its streets bear the names of Minnesota pioneers such as Flandrau, Schoolcraft, Beltrami, and Joseph Renshaw Brown.

Lewis's last Minnesota novel, *The God-Seeker*, is set in the fictional Bois de Mortes, a settlement two hundred miles west of Fort Snelling on the Minnesota River. Lewis published his novel in 1949, the centennial year of the Minnesota Territory.

Lewis had always appreciated scenic vistas, and he compared Minnesota's rolling hills and quaint villages to those of New England.[5] He explored his home state extensively, recording his favorite vistas and publishing his accounts. He was almost ashamed to say he had traveled throughout New England in search of beauty when his own state had every bit as much to offer.

The view of the St. Croix valley was his favorite, and he especially enjoyed Highway 8 as it wound down picturesque bluffs into the town of Taylors Falls. Ranked second was the view of the Leaf Mountains in Otter Tail County, particularly the panorama of fifty lakes within twenty miles of Inspiration Peak. The Root River valley in Fillmore and Houston counties was another favorite; Lewis claimed that there was room enough for eleven thousand poets to contemplate the gently rolling hills. He also was attracted to the Mississippi River bluffs from Red Wing to La Crescent, a region known as the driftless area. He also enjoyed Lake Minnetonka, the view of Lake Minnewaska from the bluffs north of Glenwood, and the town of Kandiyohi, which oddly enough reminded him of a Cape Cod village even though the town bordered no large body of water.

He used the *WPA Guide to Minnesota* for his tours and implored his friends, who had traveled Europe, to sample the Leaf Mountains instead of the Alps. He was proud of his Minnesota and was shocked to learn that most Minnesotans knew relatively little about their state.

When he wrote a travel article for the *Minneapolis Tribune* in 1942, Lewis never had ventured up the north shore of Lake Superior and he admitted this; as a result, he wasn't able to include that area in his writings on Minnesota beauty. In August 1942, the article was reprinted in an outdoor magazine, *The Conservation Volunteer*, and Lewis left Minneapolis for an outing at Hungry Jack Lake on the Gunflint Trail. He immediately fell in love with the area and returned to the same spot two years later.

Lewis, always devoted to his native soil, kept a journal describing daily experiences in Minnesota. His diary, which often was humorous, included Burma Shave slogans along the highway and tombstone readings in local cemeteries.

In 1947 Lewis launched a final effort to come home to Minnesota. Although he never was captivated by historical fiction, he long had been interested in Minnesota's history and people, and decided to drop anchor in St. Paul. Working with little rest in the archives of the Minnesota State Historical Society, he researched the state's history, wrote about real people, but playfully injected his own fictionalized accounts.

Lewis could have fun only in his fiction, however, for he had come home too late to be accepted. He had tried several times as a young man to settle in and near Minnesota, but serious altercations with friends and neighbors made that impossible. He could contrive homes for all the characters in his novels, but the Nobel Prize-winning author could not find a home of his own. So he went on searching while he criticized others who had turned their backs to their native soil. He summed up his feelings on the last page of his novel *The God-Seeker*:

> It is an illusion that the haze of the far-off hills is bluer and more romantic.
>
> In every state of the union, as in Minnesota, we have historical treasures small and precious and mislaid. It is admirable that we should excavate Ur of the Chaldees and study the guilds of Brabant, but for our own dignity, knowledge and plain tourist interest, we might also excavate Urbana of the Illinois and investigate the first labor organization of the Bronx.[6]

1

Sauk Centre

And she saw that Gopher Prairie was merely an enlargement of all the hamlets which they had been passing. Only to the eyes of a Kennicott was it exceptional. The huddled low wooden houses broke the plains scarcely more than would a hazel thicket. The fields swept up to it, past it. It was unprotected and unprotecting; there was no dignity in it nor any hope of greatness. Only the tall red grain-elevator and a few tinny church-steeples rose from the mass. It was a frontier camp. It was not a place to live in, not possibly, not conceivably.[1]

EDWIN WHITEFIELD, noted artist and writer, was temporarily residing in Kandotta (now Kandota) Township in 1854.[2] Whitefield, born in England, was impressed with the area and longed to establish a townsite and build a dam on the Ashley River and Fairy Lake to provide power for a sawmill and gristmill. Whitefield planned to paint the surrounding countryside and take his paintings to the East to promote the land and bring settlers to his townsite.

As Whitefield worked on his canvases, another settler, Alexander Moore, commenced construction of a dam on the Sauk River in June 1857. By 1860 a sawmill and gristmill were in operation. The birth of Sauk Centre was inevitable.

When Sinclair Lewis was born on February 7, 1885, Sauk Centre was still a raw prairie town. Only twenty-three years before, during the Sioux Uprising of 1862, a stockade had been constructed around the home and store of settler Solomon Pendergast, and a company of soldiers was stationed within.[3] During that same decade, a flood washed away Moore's dam, gristmill, and sawmill, and the prospects of rebuilding waned. Although many other buildings soon were erected, Sauk Centre did not officially become a village until 1876; so young Lewis did experience life on the frontier prairie.[4]

Sinclair Lewis Birthplace: 811 Sinclair Lewis Avenue, Sauk Centre, MN. The author was born in this house Feb. 7, 1885. Photograph by Catherine Keller, 1979.

E. L. Kells, a former resident of Sauk Centre and acquaintance of Sinclair Lewis, recalls the village as it appeared to the author:

> Sauk Lake and Sauk River were big items in town to all boys. The original dam was built by Alexander Moore to power his mill, the mill building still stands in part. Moore was some guy, Ben D[uBois] has told me much about him. The Main Street bridge, at the dam, was a favorite swimming and diving spot. Sauk Lake is the flooded bed of the Sauk River, in essence the mill pond back of the dam. The river, prior to damming, is typical of many midwestern streams in that its bed was much wider than present day flow would require. This great width was quite likely cut by glacial runoff during the last melting about 12,000 years ago. Thus the major part of the present town (and almost all the old town) was on a plateau somewhat lower than the immediate adjacent country. This

can be noted when leaving town in any direction, a climb is involved. The town had three major bridges over the river, that at the dam on Main Street, the Third Street bridge and the "Mile Bridge" which was about a mile SE of the center of town on the road to Melrose.[5]

The geography of Sauk Centre undoubtedly suited its adolescent population, which swarmed into its lakes, rivers, hills, and valleys. The railroad had come to Sauk Centre, and it mesmerized young Lewis, who quickly adopted it as part of his natural playground.
Kells continues:

> Fairy Lake is a natural lake with no outlet, fed largely by swamps and runoff from the north. The Hoboken Creek swimming hole was near "Stone Arch," a single-arch Great Northern Railroad bridge beautifully built of hewn stone blocks. It had great acoustics for shouting and was an exciting place to be when a train went overhead, particularly when the 3 o'clock Flyer (aka GN's Oriental Limited) went through town like a bat out of hell. Both the GN and NP had good depots at that time with, I'm quite sure, both men's and women's waiting rooms, each with its own pot bellied stove. Both had water tanks for the locomotives and the NP had coaling facilities. The GN had extensive siding and a freight unloading dock with derrick (good climbing). At the intersection of the GN and NP was a signal tower manned by a gent who had levers for switches and semaphores, etc. A visit up there was strictly excruciating. The GN had a spur that took off to the north near this tower, called the "K" line since it formed the leg of a **K** with the GN main line and the NP. The K line took off across the prairies, passing near Fairy Lake, its right of way had early mayflowers and gave an excellent view back across the foot of the lake to town. Hiking along these tracks was great sport, walking rails, picking up spikes and flares, etc. Also climbing cars on the sidings.

It was in this same Hoboken "Crick" (the children refused to enunciate *creek*) that young Lewis almost lost his life.[6] The swimming hole, though generally shallow, was rife with drop-offs. Lewis, who could not swim, one day attempted to impress his brother Claude but slipped into deep water. None of the preoccupied children realized what had happened until Al Pendergast, an observer, rushed to the boys with news of the accident. Claude leaped from the springboard

Hoboken Hill, Sauk Centre. This hill served as Sinclair Lewis's playground in the 1890s and was especially popular in winter for sliding. Photograph by Catherine Keller, 1979.

and rescued his frightened brother, whose brilliant literary career surely would have ended before it had begun.

Young Lewis was always an outsider. He was constantly at the heels of his older brother and his brother's companions, and his gullibility made him ever the target of jokes.[7] Often, when he was in the water pretending to swim, the older boys would tie his clothes in knots and vanish. One of the older youths was even assigned the task of devising methods for ditching him, and very often Lewis returned home alone.

Claude, seven years Harry's senior, was the second son of Edwin J. and Emma Lewis. Harry spent his entire life trying to impress Claude, and the two remained fairly close throughout their lives. An older brother, Fred, was never close to Harry because of the great difference in their ages and their contrasting occupations and characters: Harry was an erratic and imaginative writer, and Fred was a rock-ribbed and practical farmer.[8]

Lewis's father, a physician, was a well-respected figure in the community. Known invariably as "EJ," he kept an office on Main Street overlooking Sauk Centre's busiest intersection and devoted himself to

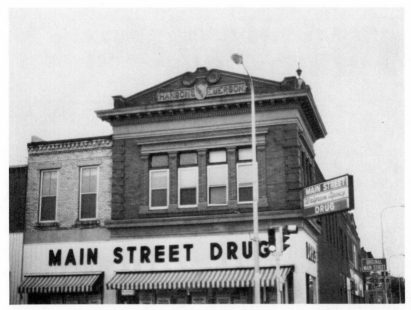

Dr. E. J. Lewis's medical office on the intersection of Main Street and S. L. Avenue. Dr. Lewis's office was located above the Main Street Drug which served as Dyer's Drug in Main Street. Photograph by Catherine Keller, 1979.

his work until his death in 1926. A staid Victorian, he imposed numerous restrictions on his sons and tolerated no rebellion. Claude was always the success, always the one who did what was expected of him, and always the one of whom EJ was most proud. If there was any jealousy on Harry's part, however, he never revealed it.

Harry perhaps was closer to his stepmother, Isabel Warner Lewis, who married Harry's father in 1892.[9] Harry's own mother, Emma Kermott Lewis, had suffered from tuberculosis. Despite Edwin Lewis's efforts to restore her health by taking her to a milder climate in the American Southwest, she died in 1891.

The Lewis children quickly accepted their stepmother. Isabel Warner was kind and ambitious. She supervised meetings of the local musical club, founded the local chapter of the Order of the Eastern Star, was an officer in the Congregational church, the Gradatim Club, and the Embroidery Club and helped found the town's first public rest room for the wives and children of visiting farmers.[10]

Lewis may have liked Grandfather Warner, Isabel's father, as much as he liked his stepmother. Young Lewis would for hours listen to Grandfather Warner spin historical tales. Their imaginative conversa-

S. L. boyhood home: 812 Sinclair Lewis Avenue. The home is now open to the public as a museum. Photograph by Catherine Keller, 1979.

Grave of Emma Kermott Lewis, Greenwood Cemetery, Sauk Centre. The real mother of Sinclair Lewis, she passed away when the youth was six years old. Photograph by Catherine Keller, 1979.

tions likely prompted Lewis to become a storyteller. In Warner, young Lewis found a hero, someone he could communicate with and someone who accepted him on his own terms.

Gray Warner, Grandfather Warner's son and Isabel Warner's brother, described his father in a letter to Claude Lewis dated February 6, 1937:

> Father was not very much of a talker to tell of his experience, but once in a while you could get him started on a particular thing. I remember he was one of the Pinkerton guards that were with Lincoln when he went through Baltimore on his way to inauguration at Washington, and was also one of Ben Butker's aides in New Orleans.
>
> Allan Pinkerton wrote a book called "The Expressman & the Detective" in which Father was quite prominent and even a picture of him with a full beard is in the book.
>
> Father was in the lumber business with Frank in Ottawa with a big yard but Pinkerton got him to come to Chicago as superintendent of his agency and then sent him to New York for a while and we all moved to Stamford, Connecticut thinking we would like to live in the east, but Pinkerton brought him back to Chicago and he was in charge there for about 20 years.

After his service with Pinkerton, Grandfather Warner worked for the American Express Company, which paid him twice the salary he had drawn with the detective agency. During the Civil War, he was a member of the Secret Service and was captured as a spy. The night before his trial, his guard fell asleep and Warner escaped, reaching the Union lines in a matter of hours. Before he worked for Pinkerton, he had served as a county sheriff.

It was in the company of his stepmother that Harry first met Ben DuBois.[11] Mrs. Lewis was visiting Mrs. Julian DuBois at the DuBois home, then located at 104 North Main Street in a section of town known as Brooklyn. As Harry and Ben sat facing each other on the lawn, Harry bet his new companion that he could eat grass like a cow and quickly proved it.

Lewis wanted desperately to be a leader, but could find no one to follow him. He would continually strive to establish friendships with the older children, but those relationships always ended in failure. He soon became a loner, if not a full-fledged rebel. There were brief friendships with Laurel Kells, John MacGibbon and Minnie Pike, and a brief flirtation with Clara Carpenter. He would roam the neighbor-

Julian DuBois House: 828 Sinclair Lewis Avenue. Ben DuBois was a child-hood companion of S. L. and the latter once ate grass to gain his friendship. Photograph by Catherine Keller, 1979.

hood in and out of mischief, and Charles McCadden, a close friend of Claude, was often his confederate in apple-stealing escapades.[12] Still, few, if any, lasting relationships materialized.

Many found Lewis unique and difficult, as evidenced by a visiting relative who recorded this story in her diary:

> When I was ten years old I was sent to spend the winter with my aunt and uncle in a little town in Minnesota. They were very strict and though I had good times and loved it when my uncle took me in the buckboard to hunt prairie chicken and I loved skating on the lake and going sleighing. I loved all that. But the evenings were so long and I was lonely. My cousin was 14 or 15 and he teased me so much that I hated him. One time he threw an open jacknife down the stairs at me but his father whipped him good for that. He became a famous writer and we grew to be good friends. You may have heard his name. It was Sinclair Lewis.[13]

Lewis finally found a devoted friend in Irving Fisher, with whom he frequently practiced running and played cribbage and chess.[14] There was never any competition between the two, and they were quick to note that they were both outsiders with common interests. Fisher was Lewis's intellectual equal, a young man with whom Lewis could discuss "deep" subjects; they relished each other's thoughts regarding philosophy and literature. For Lewis, it was exhilarating to be in the company of someone who did not make fun of him.

At school, Lewis was anything but a model student. He never fraternized with other students, and he had absolutely no interest in sports. Seldom did he apply himself to his schoolwork, and he was not outstanding in any subject, including spelling and English.

His eighth-grade report card characterized his scholastic achievements: a grammar grade of 75, a spelling grade of 70; in a class of eighteen, he finished seventeenth. Nonetheless, his teachers were impressed by the journal he kept, and his parents were mildly amused by this entry: "$2.98 for d. foolishness." His teachers always remembered his 1898 escapade, when he ran away from home to enlist in the Spanish-American War, only to be intercepted by his father in nearby Melrose.

During the summer of 1901, when he was sixteen, Lewis went to work for the *Sauk Centre Avalanche*, one of two newspapers in town. It was not a good job—he wasn't paid—but he hoped to gain journalistic experience by surveying the town, its people, and trivial events.[15]

Two summers later he returned to the *Avalanche* as a paid employee, receiving five dollars per week, six if he performed well.[16] Just how well he did is open to speculation, for the position lasted only two weeks; he gathered news, subscriptions, and bills, and devoted his remaining time to writing.

After the town's first hotel, the Sauk Centre House, burned down, Richard L. Palmer constructed the Palmer House on the same site in 1901.[17] For two weeks during the summer of 1902, Harry worked there as a night clerk from six in the evening until six in the morning, earning five dollars per week plus room and board.[18]

Sauk Centre was served by a dozen trains per day, and the Palmer was always filled with salesmen.[19] One salesman asked Lewis to wake him at two in the morning so he could catch the three o'clock train. The dozing clerk overslept but did wake the man to inform him that he had missed his train. Lewis returned to the Palmer House the following summer in the same capacity but was slightly more adept in his work. The Palmer House served as Lewis's model for the Minniemashie House in *Main Street*.

In addition to his labors at the Palmer House during the summer of 1902, Lewis worked for C. F. Hendryx at the *Sauk Centre Herald*, a rival of the *Avalanche*.[20] Again earning experience but no salary, he served as typesetter, but it was during this period of employment at the *Herald* that he published his first written work, a graduation story that appeared in the newspaper June 5, 1902.

Lewis may have been less than enthusiastic over some of the more arduous tasks at the newspaper, but he was infatuated with the boss's daughter, Myra, who was his own age.[21] His affection for Myra Hendryx would haunt him throughout his adolescence, and even though he courted several other eligible young ladies, he did so hoping only to make Myra jealous. Though Myra considered Lewis a nice young man, she never was attracted to him and, throughout their one-sided relationship, the smitten bachelor experienced the pain of rejection.

Sauk Centre was a wonderful place to court a young lady. On moonlit nights, Lewis and Myra would rent a boat from Nels Orvaar at the livery and float like lilies across the rippling waters of Sauk Lake. The lights of Sauk Centre twinkled in the black water, and if the youngsters rowed near the Main Street bridge, they could just make out Solomon Pendergast's elegant mansion, which watched over the village like a citadel.

Business was always good at the *Herald*; so good, in fact, that the newspaper purchased its rival, the *Avalanche*. Yet the C. F. Hendryx residence was anything but elegant and sat next to the railroad tracks where noisy trains traveled en route to a nearby stockyard.

Lewis left Myra and Sauk Centre in 1902 to attend Oberlin College in Ohio. When he returned in the summer he was full of revolutionary ideas regarding politics and religion and was most eager to discuss his convictions. Fisher, too, was evolving, and the two young philosophers rallied together, developing new theories and testing old ones.

The most serious rift in the Lewis family occurred when Sinclair began weighing the virtues of Congregationalism against those of Episcopalianism. The family had always taken pride in being staunch Congregationalists, and Lewis's father had forbidden members of the family ever to look outside their own religion. Suddenly his upstart son had rejected the family faith and was exploring alternatives. Edwin Lewis grew angry and attempted to convince his son that Congregationalism was the answer. Sinclair ignored his father's advice and attended services at the Church of the Good Samaritan Episcopal Church on Main Street. He had been overwhelmed by religious zeal and was a true believer, embracing a faith other than his family's.

Fisher quickly followed suit, and the two met daily to discuss their conversions. Content only briefly, they soon grew weary of tradition and began looking beyond the doctrines of the church. Those attending Sunday morning services saw less and less of the two young men who now were drifting toward agnosticism. A stunned E. J. Lewis realized he was losing his grip on his son.

Although Lewis turned his back on religion, he never lost interest in its principles. He and Fisher were eager to learn all they could about philosophy and religion, and they seldom missed a lecture at the Grand Army of the Republic Hall or the Sauk Centre Community Club. They frequented the Bryant Library, where they pursued the best in literature, and attended the Main Street Theater, where they witnessed a sampling of vaudeville.

By summer's end, E. J. Lewis was only too eager to see his son off to Yale, where he hoped Harry might be enlightened by principles of logic. Harry pleaded with his father to send him to Harvard, but to no avail, and the boy was bound for Connecticut.

Lewis returned summers, but upon graduation from Yale did not return to Sauk Centre for eight years. During this period he matured, changing from a boy haunted by conflicting convictions to a man eager to put concrete ideas to work for him. In addition to scores of short stories and articles, he published three novels: *Hike and the Aeroplane* (1912), *Our Mr. Wrenn* (1914), and *The Trail of the Hawk* (1915).

In 1914 he married Grace Hegger, and he was eager to show her his

Bryant Library, corner 5th and Main Sts., Sauk Centre. The library has 26,000 books and most visitors who come to town read Main Street. Photo by Catherine Keller, 1979.

boyhood home. In 1916 Lewis and Grace decided to come to Sauk Centre so the author could write his novel *The Job* in the solitude of his hometown.[22] For Grace it was her first visit to Sauk Centre, but Lewis felt just as much a stranger, having been away for so long.

They were not comfortable in the E. J. Lewis home. Whenever their mail was taken up to them, it already had been opened. Once Grace was forced to come to breakfast against her wishes. Convinced they could have no privacy in his parents' home, Lewis threatened to leave if he and his wife were not given more freedom.

Despite these problems, Dr. and Mrs. Lewis were proud to have their son home and sponsored a dinner party for the couple so that friends in the community could meet their daughter-in-law. E. J. Lewis passed around the current issue of *Cosmopolitan*, which featured a serial by his son. When guests asked how much he had been paid for the contribution, they were told fifteen hundred dollars. A few guests immediately began computing the salary that amounted to, and one woman asked Lewis how much he had given his wife. The younger Lewises were shocked that everything in the small town was measured by dollars and cents.

They were invited to card parties and taken on picnics to Sauk and Fairy lakes. Lewis would stop by the Commercial Club, the corner drugstore, and the library. Grace and Harry visited Dr. Lewis at his office—an office very similar to that of Dr. Kennicott in *Main Street.*

The picnics, parties, and solitary walks about town, however, were not enough to satisfy a serious writer, and Lewis grew ever more restless. He longed to get back to *The Job*, but he knew he couldn't write at home because he lacked privacy. His father, who wished to spare him from paying rent, suggested he take a spare room in his office.

Lewis rejected the offer, fearful he would be afforded as little privacy in the office as at home. Instead he rented a bare office over Rowe's Hardware Store on Main Street. He borrowed a table and chair, for he required nothing else, and adopted a rigorous writing schedule. Writing day in and day out, with little time for recreation, he began work on his fourth novel.

When E. J. Lewis announced that he and his wife were leaving Sauk Centre for a two-week vacation and leaving the house to the young couple, Harry was shocked. The gesture may have been his father's way of permitting them to be introduced to the town on their own, or it may have been merely an act of kindness. They entertained and enjoyed two wonderful weeks without parental supervision.

Having made much progress on *The Job*, Lewis grew weary of Sauk

Centre and purchased an automobile, which neither he nor his wife knew how to operate, and a tent that fit neatly over the top of the five-passenger touring car. The book would be completed a year later in Duluth during a visit to his friend, writer Claude Washburn. He had wanted to complete the book in Sauk Centre, but there was little in his hometown that appealed to him. He was no longer like most people, nor had he ever been; as quickly as they had come, the Lewises left Sauk Centre. It would be another four years before they returned.

The real bombshell was the publication of *Main Street* in 1920. In this novel, which depicted small-town America, Lewis used real people as characters, and it was obvious to many just who these persons really were. The town had been under the microscope of a radical, and the citizens considered their lifestyles under attack.

Fear and anger were not limited to Sauk Centre, for the book unleashed a series of seismic waves across the entire country. Catholic parishioners in Melrose, Minnesota, were warned not to read any books by Sinclair Lewis and that anyone committing such an act would go straight to hell.[23]

Book banning has always been a boon for book sales, and people rushed to their favorite bookstore to procure a copy. Even those who hadn't read the book knew it by reputation.

Was Lewis striking back at Sauk Centre for dealing him a lonely boyhood or was he merely placing a lifestyle in perspective? He had always been fond of his place of birth, as evidenced by what he wrote in the 1931 *Sauk Centre Annual*: "I could have been born and reared in no place in the world where I would have had more friendliness. . . . It was a good time, a good place, and a good preparation for life."[24]

How delightful his boyhood really was is open to speculation. With the exception of the faithful Irving Fisher, Lewis enjoyed no lasting relationships, and when the Fishers moved from Sauk Centre while Lewis was still a young man, there was no one to whom he could turn. Brothers Claude and Fred were married and pursued their own careers. Myra Hendryx never had been fond of him, and even her brother Jim, whom he had once counted as a friend, was no longer available and was contemplating a writing career of his own. Religious affiliations were out of the question, for he had abandoned his faith. He always would be fond of Hoboken Hill and Creek and Sauk and Fairy lakes, but he had grown weary of the townspeople and Sauk Centre's social institutions.

One Sauk Centre resident and acquaintance of Sinclair Lewis recapitulates her feelings regarding the author's explosion in print: "I think his 'Main Street' gave him the chance he always wanted, i.e. to make Sauk Centre suffer for the lonely, intolerable boyhood he had spent here."[25]

There was no room for a free spirit in the community, especially for Sinclair Lewis. The town felt betrayed by a former citizen who had attacked its families and institutions. E. J. Lewis was ashamed of his son's book and was caught in the middle since he was fond both of his town and his son.

Former Sauk Centre resident E. L. Kells recalls the town's reaction to *Main Street*:

> My recollection of the town's reaction to "Main Street" is fairly clear though I was pretty young and not too analytical. A number of people I remember commenting on it were actively unhappy, and this must include Ben's [DuBois] statements—the years have mellowed him and broadened him, he used to be more sharply critical than now—not unkindly but more pointed. My mother was not pleased with the book and, as was her SOP, she said so. The composite reaction was predictable when viewed broadly: here was a guy who was less than loved by his fellows; who had gone away to an Eastern school and who had never developed and therefore couldn't maintain a friendly warm relationship with the people and the town; but who deigned to portray some of the aspects of the then small towns with sufficient accuracy as to scrape a few nerves. This is not to suggest he was wholly right in his perceptions and I've always felt he was one sided in that a town such as Sauk Centre is just one hell of a fine place to grow up in and live and there are an enormous number of compensations for the real and imagined deficiencies.[26]

Lewis did "scrape a few nerves," and the barriers erected between him and the community were never completely torn down. It was now too late to consider coming home to live in Sauk Centre, for old hangouts like Emerson's Drug, the Palmer House, and the Main Street Theater were as distant from his world as were the fictional Dyer's Drug, Minniemashie House, and Rosebud Theater. With the exception of a few acquaintances who stood by him during the turmoil, Sauk Centre was no more home to him than was an island in the Pacific.

Though Lewis never was completely accepted by the townsfolk, attitudes toward him changed for a couple of reasons. E. L. Kells elaborates:

As to the relatively recent canonization of Lewis, it would be too simple and not correct to attribute a major portion of its motivation to a desire to exploit the accident of his being born here. Since the writing of "Main Street" there have been enormous changes in the outlook of people everywhere, largely brought on by the astronomical advances in communication. Thus people have broadened, their outlooks and actions and concerns have changed, and, in effect, Lewis's book became obsolete. Concurrently over these years the people who knew Lewis and maybe ran a temperature over his book, aged, mellowed, diminished in influence and many of them demised. So by time it was decided the town had an under-recognized celebrity in the wings the people available to consider this and act on it were not at all those who had the early contacts and views and, in fact, the views of these late actors were predicated on criteria light years removed from those of such as my mother and father and their contemporaries during the Lewis period. A classical case of post-atomic people viewing a pre-atomic situation.

Despite the bitterness expressed over *Main Street*, the citizens of Sauk Centre did honor Lewis with a reception at the Palmer House in 1920, shortly after publication of the novel.[27] During the course of the dinner, one Sauk Centre resident queried Lewis about his opinion of Eugene Debs, controversial labor leader and founder of the American Socialist Party. Lewis compared him to Christ. All those present at the table were shocked; the head of a wealthy, respected banker mechanically wagged back and forth like a berserk, racing pendulum.

Although the men and women of the prairie town considered Lewis blind to the good life they were living, Lewis himself felt he had been fair to them. He was not criticizing small towns; he was criticizing America and was quick to voice this opinion in his own defense: "If I seem to have criticized prairie villages, I have certainly criticized them no more than I have New York, or Paris, or the great universities."[28]

Yet, as author Barnaby Conrad points out, "Mr. Lewis always managed to hurt the people he loved most."[29] The prairie people were his people, and they were certainly the people he loved most. Throughout his life, wherever he traveled in the world, he reminisced about Sauk Centre:

> I find myself thinking of its streets and its people and the familiar friendly faces when I am on the great avenues of New York, or Paris, or Berlin, or Stockholm; when I am in

the little stone hilly villages of Italy, or sun-basking villas in Spain, or the yellow ancient temples of Athens. To me, forever, *ten miles* will not be a distance in the mathematical table, but slightly more than the distance from Sauk Centre to Melrose. To me, forever, though I should live to be ninety, the direction *west* will have nothing in particular to do with California or the Rockies; it will be that direction which is to the left—towards Hoboken Hill—if you face the house of Dr. E. J. Lewis.[30]

Lewis could never quite remove the shackles that bound him to Sauk Centre. The publication of *Main Street* had branded him, both at home and abroad; anyone who had gulped the dust of the prairie, dropped anchor in a small town, or believed in the virtues of the American way of life, was suspicious that Lewis looked toward home but never settled there.

After the reception at the Palmer House, Lewis dropped in on old friends and roamed the streets of his childhood. He seemed to desire the conformity of Sauk Centre, wanting its gentry to accept him for what he was, and it hurt him when he found his acceptance impossible. He had inflicted a gaping wound on Sauk Centre, but the town also had injured him. As a young boy, he had been rejected by his peers at school, rejected at love, considered odd, and he had been forced to take refuge in his room at home or in the company of his fellow recluse, Irving Fisher. Reflecting on his boyhood, he remembered only the loneliness that had grown out of his rejection. Misunderstood, he would go away in search of a new home, the elusive utopia he had failed to find in a lonely boyhood.

Lewis became accustomed to travel—especially traveling alone—whether it was one of his numerous trips to the Twin Cities to attain a degree of independence or the reckless wanderings of an outsider bent on becoming a part of a communal experiment. Travel provided him an outlet for escape, an opportunity to thwart rejection and begin anew. In a letter to his brother Claude dated May 14, 1933, he persuaded Claude to allow his daughter Virginia the privilege of traveling abroad:

> And now is the time for her to travel. As you know, I have traveled a good deal, and I assure you that out of my trips as a kid—such as the Panama adventure and cattle-boat to Europe—I got a hundred times as much as I could possibly get now, even were I to travel to the heart of China. A youngster is strong, flexible; he, or she, can stand discomfort,

poor food, sitting up all night, with relish. And being fresh to the world, he or she sees so much more freshly and acutely, gets so much more kick, and so vastly many more new and valuable ideas. It's the only time to travel instead of, as most people do, waiting till they are middle-aged and prosperous and can afford it—but also cannot really enjoy it.

As Lewis globe-trotted far from the hornet's nest he had stirred in Sauk Centre, his stepmother became gravely ill.[31] She died June 14, 1921, while Lewis and Grace were in England. It took more than three weeks for the attending physician's letter to reach the author in Cornwall.

It was obvious that E. J. Lewis could not take care of his house himself, so a neighboring family, the Roterts, who had always been fond of the Lewises, moved into the house to care for him.[32] Mrs. Rotert served as EJ's housekeeper. Mr. Rotert, a conductor on the Great Northern Railway through Sauk Centre, was a gentle man who was fond of children, but his job kept him away much of the time.

In 1924, after a trip into the Canadian wilderness to research a novel with his brother, Lewis returned to Sauk Centre for a ten-day respite with his father.[33] During his brief stay, he penned an enthusiastic review of Carl Van Vechtan's *The Tattooed Countess*, which had

Grave of Isabel Warner Lewis, Greenwood Cemetery, Sauk Centre. She founded several clubs, was an officer in the Congregational Church, and helped found the town's first public rest room for wives and children of visiting farmers. Photograph by Catherine Keller, 1979.

appeared in the *Saturday Review of Literature*. After leaving Sauk Centre, he paused in St. Paul before returning East.

Whenever Lewis returned to Sauk Centre in the 1920s, he ritually would drop by George O'Gara's garage on South Main Street.[34] Lewis never had been popular with most of the town's citizens, but within the walls of O'Gara's he was always accepted. Companions who never had shocked easily welcomed their native son home with drink, merriment, and nostalgia. Prohibition was in full swing, but O'Gara always provided liquor and good company. O'Gara had known Lewis for years and was one of the few who never had been offended by his attack on the small towns.

Sinclair found great delight in inviting out-of-state companions to Sauk Centre, especially when he could show them the seamier side of town, as he did with the Reverend Earl Blackman, whom he had met in Kansas City while researching *Elmer Gantry*. Lewis and his guests would always commence the evening by dropping by O'Gara's, and the proprietor would immediately become engaged in a telephoning marathon.

Within half an hour, a group of Lewis's favorite people would be assembled at the garage, and they then would head out of town in their automobiles to Stratton's speakeasy, a favorite night spot. It was a short jaunt out County 17 beyond the cemetery; the night would be broken only by the light of an occasional farmhouse and the moon overhead. At the intersection with Highway 13, they would turn toward Melrose and pull up to an isolated farmhouse. Ray Stratton's sanctuary was well outside the city limits and was completely safe since the town marshal and the county sheriff would frequently attend the party in Lewis's company.

Frequently at Stratton's there was a girl who could swear so effectively Lewis relished the prospect of simply hearing her. He wanted his friends to hear her too, and when the non-Minnesotans would appear even mildly amused, he would give way to laughter. The liquor at Stratton's was "top shelf," and the Hudson Super-Six that he stocked cost two dollars a pint. Business at the farmhouse flourished, and Stratton was described by the Lewis bunch as looking like "a well-fed priest."

After O'Gara sold the garage and opened a restaurant on one of the town's busiest intersections, Lewis continued to visit him. They would dash off to Stratton's as before, but the good old days at the garage were behind them. A link with the past had died, and it just wasn't the same. Rocks Woodkey, whom Lewis had known since childhood, operated a blacksmith shop near the restaurant, and Lewis sometimes would stop by for a visit.

In 1926 Lewis was relaxing on a remote island in Minnesota's Rainy Lake when word reached him that his father, not quite seventy-eight years old, had died August 29.[35] E. J. Lewis had never forgiven his son for *Main Street*, and although they had continued to shake hands and embrace during visits, the act had been mechanical. Lewis had never consciously meant to hurt his father; in fact, he thought that he had bestowed an honor upon him. But through the doctor's eyes, his son had libeled his own birthplace. Lewis now felt remorse that he had been considered a traitor in the house of his father—the father who had never approved of his writing career and who had hoped that he would become a physician like his brother Claude.

Liberal Kansas City minister L. M. Birkhead, a Unitarian and agnostic, accompanied Lewis when he returned to Sauk Centre to attend his father's funeral. The pair rented rooms in the Palmer House, and there was much gossip about the return of the prodigal son. Birkhead, whom no one in the town recognized, was informed by the village barber that Lewis had coerced his wife to write his novels for him. Though Birkhead found the incident amusing, he remained mute.

The day of the funeral, Lewis drank heavily, partly in mourning for his father and partly for the grief he had caused him. Before leaving Sauk Centre, he handed the Roterts a check and remarked that, regardless of the amount, it should have been more. In another impulsive gesture, he gave his cherished Buick to his brother Fred, perhaps as a token of the brotherhood that was never theirs.

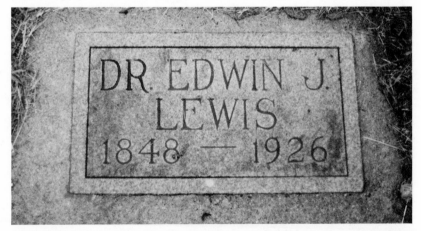

Grave of Dr. E. J. Lewis, Greenwood Cemetery, Sauk Centre. He exhibited little toleration for rebellion. His death in 1926 brought Sinclair home to Sauk Centre. Photograph by Catherine Keller, 1979.

Although his father was dead, Lewis could not forget him. Often he had resented his father for his precision and punctuality, but never had he lost respect for him. The inner conflict that raged because of this pitted Lewis the rebel against Lewis the puritan in a never-ending struggle. He had never been like other boys, nor did he want to be, and he was unable to cope with his father, who pushed him toward conformity.

On May 14, 1928, Lewis married American journalist Dorothy Thompson in London.[36] Filling the void between his breakup with Grace Hegger and his marriage to Thompson, a dejected Lewis had hired Louis Florey as his secretary. Florey had served as stenographer, drinking companion, valet, and full-time babysitter.[37] He retained Florey's services after his second marriage. Florey had been a good listener and faithful attendant, and Lewis desperately needed a friend.

In the mid-1930s, Lewis returned again to Sauk Centre, bringing Florey with him.[38] It was a nostalgic trip for Lewis, who delighted in showing Florey his favorite swimming hole on Hoboken Creek and the arch where his brother Claude had carved his initials nearly a half-century earlier. The arch was still there, and so were the initials.

Many of the treasured landmarks still remained, but gone were his family and friends. His old drinking partner, George O'Gara, was no longer in Sauk Centre, but he recalled how O'Gara had sold him his first car, the receptions the garageman had thrown for him, and the thrill-packed rides out to Stratton's. The Gentses' Clothing Store brothers had vanished, and Bill Parker, his postman friend who frequently had joined him at O'Gara's, was gone. His family, too, was gone: father, mother, and stepmother deceased and brother Claude in St. Cloud. There was Fred, of course, but the two brothers remained distant. On the streets Lewis encountered blank stares, for few people recognized him. He was lonely and lost, for he had severed all ties with the village of his birth. He had always been alienated, but the people he had antagonized, the people he loved most, had always been there before, and even their scorn had somehow served as a source of consolation. Sauk Centre was now an alien place inhabited by strangers.

Nonetheless, Lewis returned to Sauk Centre several times. On May 17, 1942, Lewis, who then was living in Minneapolis, delivered a speech at the First Congregational Church of Sauk Centre, commemorating its seventy-fifth anniversary.[39] Perhaps by returning to the church he once had rejected he was compromising with his dead father—attempting to make amends by honoring his memory.

Lewis now scrutinized the town through older and wiser eyes. There was no longer any need to shock anyone, nor did he desire to. Most of the people he had chronicled in·*Main Street* had died, and their sons and daughters were not eager to bear a grudge. Sauk Centre had undergone many changes; old mores had given way to newer ones, and traditional values had been shed. He had been a pioneer among writers who depicted small towns in their nakedness, but such towns had since been dissected many times over. Most people who had rejected this criticism now understood that changes had been necessary. *Main Street* had been merely a catalyst, an eye-opener but not the great awakening.

In January 1946, Lewis was summoned to Sauk Centre for his brother Fred's funeral.[40] He remarked to friends that poor Fred had lived his entire life without ever having left town (he had also resided in Bertha, Minnesota). Lewis may have been envious. He may have found fame and fortune, but his wanderlust had forced him to become a perpetual nomad. Fred, however, had remained in Sauk Centre and had always had a place to call home. Fred once remarked that he felt sorry for Harry because he had never hunted or fished or done the things that most people do.

Lewis's final visit to Sauk Centre occurred in October 1947, when he attended a meeting with the chamber of commerce with his servant, Joseph Hardrick.[41] Lewis addressed the banquet audience, which was honoring five "old-timers" who had been in business for more than fifty years.

There was absolutely nothing to keep him in Minnesota—or the country for that matter. In 1949 he planned a trip to Europe in a last-ditch effort to find his elusive peace of mind. He realized he did not want to go alone, and in a letter to his brother Claude, he induced him to join him:

> Mrs. Powers and I shall be leaving for Europe again between September 1st and September 15th, but this time go the Northern way, with about 2½ weeks in England, a week in Holland, a few days in Belgium, a week in Paris, about 2½ weeks in the rest of France, a few days in Switzerland, then into Italy, and to Milan, Venice, Florence, Rome, Naples— very roughly, twelve weeks from New York to Naples.
>
> Would you like to go along? The trouble is that, with many steamers destroyed in the war, the accommodations are limited, and have to be engaged months ahead. *I would have to know by ten days from now—by June 23—at the latest—whether you were going. So think fast and let me know.*

That Lewis was lonely there can be little doubt. Both of his marriages had failed. He had no one else to whom to turn but his brother. If returning to Sauk Centre was impossible, then perhaps by traveling with his brother he could take a bit of Sauk Centre with him. Lewis continued:

> From Florence we would take a car and go out and see Assisi, Parugia, Todi, Urbino, and some towns in the sharp mountainous Abruzzi—very much off the beaten tourist's trail.
>
> After Naples, Mrs. Powers and I shall stay in Italy all winter. We would be settled down, and I'll be working, and you would not be interested. So that, roughly, some time in December you would either sail back by yourself from Naples, or you might prefer to fly back, in which case you would fly from Rome to Paris, then from there to NY. Exact details of this return we would arrange after we got to' Europe, but the sailing over I must arrange here immediately. We'd probably be taking a Cunarder from NY to England.

Lewis vouched for Mrs. Powers and assured his brother that she would be an ideal traveling companion:

> She enjoys everything, never complains about anything, will talk or shut up as you prefer.

In the end, Mrs. Powers, because of a problem with her eyes, was unable to accompany Lewis. Claude did go along, partly because he had always wanted to travel in Europe and partly because, despite their differences, he relished his brother's company. Claude returned to the United States in early 1950, while Harry stayed abroad.

On January 10, 1951, Harry Sinclair Lewis died in Italy while undergoing an attack of delirium tremens. In a letter to Isabel and Virginia Lewis dated January 11, 1951, Mrs. C. B. (Helen) Lewis, Claude Lewis's second wife, related the news of Sinclair's death:

> Last evening—after all the papers and radios had sent out the information, the following message came from the State Department:
>
> ["] Department regrets inform you according message from American Embassy Rome Sinclair Lewis Died January 10 Embassy requests instructions by Cable whether Burial Rome or Shipment us ["]—Attorney's name and signature.
>
> This morning we heard over the radio, Sinclair's request

had been to be cremated and the ashes be sent to his brother Claude to be buried on the grave lot at Sauk Centre.

A nice message from the Chamber of Commerce at Sauk Centre to your Dad and no doubt something will be worked out—when instructions and further information is received here.

The funeral was held in Sauk Centre, and author Frederick Manfred, whom Lewis had once befriended, delivered the eulogy.[42] Claude was astonished to discover that his brother had willed his ashes home instead of requesting a burial in Italy. "For all his agnosticism he wanted to be buried in Sauk Centre. It surprised me a little. But it shows he had a lot of love for the old place."[43]

At the memorial service held in the local high school, the master of ceremonies appeared on stage with what appeared to be a large gift-wrapped wedding present.[44] No one there could guess what the parcel contained, and many were surprised to learn that it was merely a prop used to raise Frederick Manfred's manuscript to match the orator's great height.

Another incident occurred when, as a result of a faulty signal, the curtains opened to reveal the astonished mixed octet, which had just concluded its singing. The singers were caught in open disarray, and many members of the musical ensemble could not help but giggle. Innocent laughter swept through the congregation as a startled employee hurriedly closed the curtains. One cannot help but wish that this wave of irrepressible merriment, coming at such a solemn moment, during which Lewis's ashes reposed in an Italian urn in the vestibule of the high school, would have met with the author's approval.

Lewis's ashes were laid next to the bodies of his father, mother, and stepmother in the family plot in Greenwood Cemetery. His own stone modestly bears the inscription: "Author of Main Street." Surrounding his own ashes were the remains of the people who became in his writings the Sam Clarks, the Dave Dyers, the Jackson Elders, the Chester Dashaways, the Harry Haydocks, the Vida Sherwins, the Guy Pollocks, and the Ella Stowbodys.

As Claude Lewis crouched and lowered the urn, the warm ashes clashed with the cold January air and produced a vapor; it seemed to some that Sinclair Lewis had materialized to catch a fleeting glimpse of the town of his boyhood.[45] The apparition was hallucinatory, but with the placement of the ashes the man they called Red Lewis was home at last.

The Sinclair Lewis grave in Greenwood Cemetery. "For all his agnosticism he wanted to be buried in Sauk Centre." Photograph by Catherine Keller, 1979.

SINCLAIR LEWIS SITES IN SAUK CENTRE

1. Sinclair Lewis birthplace: 811 Sinclair Lewis (then Third) Avenue.
2. Sinclair Lewis boyhood home: 812 Sinclair Lewis Avenue.
3. Ben DuBois residence: 818 Sinclair Lewis Avenue.
4. Dr. Julian DuBois and Ben DuBois residence: 828 Sinclair Lewis Avenue.
5. Charles McCadden residence: 925 Sinclair Lewis Avenue.
6. Palmer House: 500 Sinclair Lewis Avenue.
7. Dr. Edwin J. Lewis medical office: Southwest corner of Main Street and Sinclair Lewis Avenue, above Main Street Drug.
8. Main Street Drug: Southwest corner of Main Street and Sinclair Lewis Avenue (formerly Hanson and Emerson's Drug).
9. John MacGibbon residence: 120 North Main Street.
10. *Sauk Centre Herald* Building: Third and Main streets.
11. Sauk Centre Community Club: *Herald* Building, Third and Main streets.
12. *Sauk Centre Avalanche* Building: Fourth and Main streets (razed).
13. Solomon and O'Gara's Garage: 223 South Main Street.
14. Irving Fisher residence: Fourth and Main streets (razed).
15. Rowe's Hardware Store and Sinclair Lewis residence: Fourth and Main streets (razed).
16. Solomon Pendergast residence: 50 Main Street.
17. Solomon Pendergast and William Parker residence: 61 Main Street.
18. Main Street Theater: 319 Main Street.
19. GAR Hall: Northwest corner of Fifth and Main streets (razed).
20. Bryant Library: Corner of Fifth and Main streets.
21. Church of the Good Samaritan Episcopal Church: Corner of Sixth and Main streets.

22. Laurel Kells residence: 331 South Maple.
23. C. F. Hendryx residence: 749 Railroad Avenue.
24. Woodkey's Blacksmith Shop: Fifth and Grove Lake streets (razed).
25. O'Gara's Restaurant: Grove Lake Street and Railroad Avenue (razed).
26. First Congregational Church (now First United Church of Christ): Fifth Street South and Oak Street.
27. Fred Lewis residence: 534 Lake Street.
28. Orvaar Boat Livery: By bandstand, Sauk Lake (razed).
29. Sauk Lake: Main Street.
30. Fairy Lake: Northwest of Sauk Centre.
31. Hoboken Hill: West end of Sinclair Lewis Avenue.
32. "The Arch": On Hoboken Creek just north of Hoboken Hill and the railroad tracks.
33. Clara Carpenter residence: County Road 182 (razed).
34. Stratton's speakeasy: East out of Sauk Centre on Stearns County 17, south on 13 about one-half mile, on right. (House razed; sheds and chicken coops still standing.)
35. Sinclair Lewis gravesite: Greenwood Cemetery, east end of Sinclair Lewis Avenue.
36. Sinclair Lewis Interpretive Center: Main Street and Interstate 94.

Lewis family plot, Greenwood Cemetery, Sauk Centre. Photograph by Catherine Keller, 1979.

2

St. Cloud

I think it was mainly because remembering the railroad tracks beside the road I had thought this would be most nearly the way the Kennicotts had in the first part of the book gone from Minneapolis to Gopher Prairie. Anyway, I won and we drove through Anoka and Elk River and Big Lake and Clear Lake and St. Cloud and then through Albany and Melrose to Sauk Centre.[1]

BY THE TURN of the century, St Cloud had progressed so rapidly that its population had soared to nearly ten thousand people.[2] This rapid expansion was caused in part by the hiring of new workers for the car shops in Waite Park, the paper mill at Sartell, and the state reformatory. Modern buildings were being erected, and new factories were producing commodities not previously produced in St. Cloud. In 1895 the Business Men's Association was established by one hundred businessmen.

St. Cloud's sudden population explosion was brought about by the quarrying of granite, a rock that had been discovered in St. Cloud in 1868. Little had been done with granite with the exception of paving city streets and building bridge supports, but at the turn of the century, granite was needed for the construction of all forms of monuments. By 1910 St. Cloud ranked as the fifth most populous community in Minnesota; only twenty-five years earlier it had ranked twelfth.

Claude Lewis, Harry's brother, was one of those drawn to the granite city.[3] After receiving his Bachelor of Science from the University of Minnesota in 1900, he followed in his father's footsteps by attending Rush Medical College in Chicago. For a short period, he served as an intern in local hospitals but was soon summoned to St. Cloud as a substitute physician. He performed so well he remained permanently.

In 1907 he married Rosalie Freeman, and she joined him in St. Cloud a month after their wedding. Claude called her "Merry" be-

26

The only existing photograph of Sinclair and Claude Lewis together in St. Cloud. The photo was taken outside Claude's house at 724-4th Ave. So. Photograph courtesy Isabel Lewis Agrell and Virginia Lewis.

cause of her cheerful nature, and everyone soon came to call her Mary. Trained as a nurse, Mary was just what the good doctor ordered, and the two seldom quarreled.

Harry Lewis once informed a Duluth acquaintance that his novel *Arrowsmith* had been written about his brother Claude. Paul de Kruif, a bacteriologist, supplied most of the medical background and received twenty-five percent of the book's royalties for his services, but Claude seems to have served as a model for the book's central character.

Lewis was more than qualified to write a novel focusing on medicine, since, in addition to de Kruif's assistance, his own family had supplied many prominent physicians.[4] His father had studied medicine with the influential W. D. Fluin and had become an important physician in Sauk Centre; Harry's brother Claude had been born in Ironton, Wisconsin, where his father was practicing medicine, and went on to become a renowned physician in St. Cloud; his Grandfather Kermott, on his mother's side, was a homeopathic physician in Waterville, Minnesota; Edward and Walter Kermott, his mother's brothers, were both doctors and lived high atop a hill in a Victorian mansion in Hudson, Wisconsin; their sister Juliette married Wilder Penfield, a world-famous Montreal brain surgeon. The renowned Dr. Albert Ochsner, chief surgeon of the Augustana Hospital in Chicago, was a friend of the family, and E. J. Lewis once had served under him at Rush Medical College.[5] In New Lisbon, Wisconsin, E. J. Lewis had another good friend in dentist Harry Sinclair, for whom his author son was probably named.

During July 1908, Harry Lewis was home from Yale for the summer, and with his parents away for the Independence Day holiday, he spent three weeks with Claude and Mary in St. Cloud.[6] At his brother's house he was educated in the game of bridge, and he learned to play tennis effectively. On two occasions he watched Claude perform surgery, and there were numerous outings and picnics. Lewis settled down to serious work during this sojourn and composed a short story, "The Dawn," an essay entitled "Ladies of Shallot," and two editorials.

It was during this visit in 1908 that the two brothers had their first falling out, and sporadic arguments occurred throughout their lives, most of them caused by Harry's excessive drinking.[7] Whenever Sinclair drank, he would gradually get boisterous and accuse his older brother of ordering him around. Sometimes Harry would get drunk, storm out of the house, and head down the street to spend the night with the Charles Brigham family.

Charles Brigham, a friend of Claude's, was also a physician.[8] Fay, as he was called, had graduated from the University of Minnesota in 1901, one year after Claude, and had taken his residency in St. Mary's Hospital in Duluth. In 1903 he married Agnes Harmer of Minneapolis, became a St. Cloud physician and, in time, chief of staff at the St. Cloud City Hospital.

Brigham's father, Charles S. Brigham, had been a lifelong friend of E. J. Lewis and had moved to St. Cloud in 1878. The senior Brigham died in 1919, but his widow, Emily, continued to live next door to her son's family, and Harry would always drop in at both houses. Lewis, who had always taken a fancy to the history of the United States, was fascinated by this woman, who was a direct descendant of Aaron Burr.

Lewis's erratic, drunken behavior often would embarrass his brother and cause Claude to shy away from him.[9] Yet whenever Harry appeared in St. Cloud, Claude's wife would bring out the best of everything—china, silverware, linens, tablecloths, napkins—and prepare a fine meal. Claude was not a drinker; with the exception of table wine, he never stocked any liquor in the house. This, however, posed no obstacle for Harry, who habitually carried his own supply.

In 1916 Lewis and his wife, Grace, were in Sauk Centre visiting his parents while the author worked on *The Job*.[10] Harry, eager to introduce his wife to Claude and Mary Lewis, drove to St. Cloud, and he and Grace spent a weekend with them. The two families got on well, and Claude and Mary Lewis's three children were excited over the visit. Mary told Grace how her kitchen devices had been transformed from hospital supplies: The bandage pail with foot pedal was now a handy garbage pail, and surgeon's scissors were now a means of mincing vegetables.

With the publication of *Main Street* in 1920, Lewis frequently visited St. Cloud, where there perhaps was less friction than there was in Sauk Centre. As before, he always visited the Brighams, who found great delight in picking out Sauk Centre people who served as prototypes for the book.[11]

During the decade that followed, Lewis was quick to oblige the various women's clubs of which his sister-in-law was a member and addressed them whenever his services were requested.[12] It would have shocked St. Cloud residents to hear him say things of a complimentary nature, as they were not accustomed to this kind of Sinclair Lewis, and the tart words he did choose often embarrassed Mary.

If he was lecturing close to the home of his friend Glanville Smith, he would often drop by to await his cue to appear for the lecture. Glanville, a budding young writer, was fond of the older wordsmith, and his father and Claude Lewis were fishing pals who enjoyed excursions to the Lake of the Woods area together. While awaiting his speaking engagement, Harry would frequently sample Mrs. Smith's delicious, homemade dandelion wine and methodically drain the decanter on the sideboard.

In 1922 Lewis attended the dedication of the new St. Cloud Country Club.[13] Never one to spare adjectives, he delivered a fifteen-minute impromptu speech that embarrassed Claude and raised eyebrows. Lewis praised Englishmen because they seldom boasted of their civilization, and he criticized Americans because they did, especially those in the American West. His *Main Street* had been issued only two years before, and *Babbitt* earlier the same year, so his speech came at a time when he was still known as an angry young man bent on saving America.

The Claude Lewis house was always bustling with activity, whether it served as a place to chart a canoe trip into the Canadian wilderness, or as a place to mend a broken finger. Claude was a kind man, well-respected by patients and physicians alike, and he was instrumental in guiding young medical students in the proper direction.[14] Harry took refuge at Claude's house whenever it was convenient, as it provided him with a sense of belonging. Frequently he would repose on the front porch, abstracted, seemingly composing sentences in his mind, mumbling words to himself to adjust the rhythms and points of emphasis prior to long, lonely sessions at the typewriter.[15]

Mealtime was always a ritual in the Claude Lewis home.[16] The Lewises had a small dog that was part of the family in every sense of the word but was always a nuisance at mealtime. When family members had had enough of the barking, sniffing, scratching, and begging, one of them would go to the attic and retrieve a high chair. The dog, pacified at having won its victory, would then sit in the chair to take its place with the rest of the family.

Mrs. Lewis was a frugal mother who ran a tight household.[17] After the church dinners she helped organize, she would methodically scrape butter from the plates and take it home to the family. During the Depression, she certainly was not the only one to engage in such activity.

Both Harry and his brother hated ultimatums—especially Claude. In that way they resembled their father. Dr. Harry Clark, a friend of Claude's, recalled an incident involving E. J. Lewis, whose actions reminded him of Claude. Clark, who once had served as secretary for the county medical society, had sent out cards that read: Dues must be paid by such and such a date. EJ complied with a check but included a note of his own: "*Must* is a word that should never be used to any of the Lewises." [18]

In 1929 Claude Lewis and his partner, M. J. Kern, dissolved their partnership.[19] Claude welcomed a new partner, William L. Freeman, and quickly established the Lewis Clinic, a partnership that was to endure until 1933, when they added two more physicians, Fred H. and Philip E. Stangl, forming the Lewis-Stangl Clinic on Seventh Avenue South.

The Lewis house at 710 Fourth Avenue South was showing its years, and Claude and Mary began talking about buying or building a new one.[20] The property they owned covered more than half a block. The garage behind the house contained a loft where daughters Virginia and Isabel performed all kinds of theatricals. In the winter, Claude engineered a skating rink on the corner lot for the children and even added a slide. This space was great for minstrels and children but hardly beneficial to parents, so Claude erected a new house on the corner lot at 724 Fourth Avenue South and quickly sold the old lot for a profit.

During the 1930s, Harry Lewis came to St. Cloud often, accompanied by his second wife, Dorothy Thompson.[21] Lewis's son Wells, from his previous marriage, was also brought along. Most of the child's time was spent frolicking with the Brighams' son, Charles, Jr. (or "Bud," as he was called). Bud and Wells were the same age (thirteen in 1930) and got along well together, although Wells was considered a bit delicate and effeminate in the image of his father.

During one of Harry's visits, Claude and Mary Lewis were entertaining distinguished guests, Bishop and Mrs. Kemmerer. As a duck dinner was being served, Claude grew apprehensive over his brother's heavy drinking.[22] Harry became very drunk as the evening progressed, but he minded his manners and managed to monopolize the conversation. The Kemmerers, who did not shock easily and were well versed in the conduct of Sinclair Lewis, paid little attention to his antics. As a very embarrassed Claude looked on, Mrs. Kemmerer conversed with the author the entire evening and overlooked his obnoxious behavior.

Claude Lewis's maid from 1930 to 1937 was Katy Lang. Whenever

The Claude Lewis home at 724 4th Avenue So., St. Cloud in Spring 1941. The Lewises had the house built in 1929 on their corner lot. Photograph courtesy Isabel Lewis Agrell and Virginia Lewis.

Harry came to St. Cloud, Katy would sport her attractive black uniform. With the stage set for Harry's appearance, Claude would ring a bell and Katy would appear. Harry, drunk or sober, was always given the royal treatment, and he relished the attention accorded him by his brother's family. He was not an easy man to please, as Katy found out one morning when she entered the kitchen with orange juice and attempted to serve him. Harry refused the gesture and asked that she never do it again, explaining that he liked to strain his own.

In the mid-1930s Harry returned to St. Cloud, accompanied by his secretary, Lewis Florey.[23] Lewis was in a nostalgic mood; he first took Florey to Sauk Centre and showed him all his favorite boyhood sites and then did the same in St. Cloud, introducing him to his brother and his family. After Florey had taken in St. Cloud, Harry treated him to an excursion to the Twin Cities and then drove him home to Vermont.

In subsequent trips Lewis continued to see much of the Brighams.[24] Mrs. Brigham gave dinner parties for the writer whenever he journeyed to St. Cloud, and, whether drunk or sober, calm or irate, he was always welcome in their home. He was a celebrity and it was fashionable to show him off; but more than that, they liked him and wanted him to know it.

During one of these dinner parties, it grew late and Lewis had not arrived. The Brighams waited impatiently for their guest to arrive or to telephone to give some explanation. The evening wore on, and eventually a very drunk Lewis did appear; before all the guests, he rested his feet on the dinner table and became abusive. The guests were stunned. Was this the Sinclair Lewis they had come to honor? One by one the guests stormed out, and Mrs. Brigham was so enraged that Lewis never returned to the Brigham house.

Dr. Charles F. Brigham, Jr., recalls some of Lewis's visits to his parent's home:

> As is well established, Sinclair and his brother Claude did not get along well together and on his numerous visits to St. Cloud would seek refuge in our home following a bout with Claude. For some reason my father was patient with him. I do not think it was all the fault of Sinclair, for knowing Claude as I did, he was impossible to understand.
>
> Much of the problem was due to the overuse of alcohol which was evident on many occasions. My mother attempted to entertain for him but his behavior was erratic and he was not to be depended upon. As I remember their relationship

terminated following several unsuccessful attempts for social gatherings in St. Cloud.[25]

If Lewis was rude to some, he was very considerate of others. During the early 1930s, Stearns County could boast of another author: the young, talented Glanville Smith, who had placed a pair of essays in the *Atlantic Monthly*.[26] When the *Atlantic*'s editor, Ellery Sedgwick, dispatched Smith on a writing assignment to the Antipodes, a group of islands near New Zealand, the trip acutely interested Lewis, who was visiting St. Cloud during the summer of 1934.

One night in August, before his departure, Smith pitched dishwater out of the back door of his cottage, nearly dousing Lewis, who was standing like a specter in the gloom. Lewis had attended a dinner party farther up the lakeshore, and when he had proven too hard to handle, his host, venerated St. Cloud newspaper editor Alvah Eastman, had treated him to a ride that ended at Smith's doorstep.

Lewis was full of encouragement for the younger writer and vehemently advised Smith to shake the Stearns County dirt from his soles before it soiled him permanently.

That night another guest, Alice Brown, was seated on the porch. A children's librarian from Duluth, she was Smith's mother's cousin and was introduced to Lewis as a Duluth resident. The mere mention of Duluth touched off Lewis's animosities. Alice gallantly defended her hometown. Alice rested her defense by stating that as time went on the Lord might help to rectify some of the city's defects. Lewis responded, "Don't hope that God will rectify anything in so Godforsaken a place as Duluth."

Lewis's criticisms of Duluth were curious, for he had visited the city in 1916 and had left an impression that he was fond of the city. In 1944 he moved there, and although he traveled frequently to the East, he lived in Duluth for three years. Whether he did or did not like Duluth, in his usual manner he was testing Alice Brown and, with liquor adding to his desire for confrontation, he sought an argument.

Smith failed to shake the native soil from his soles, as Lewis had advised, but he did do some touring as a travel essayist. *Harper's* launched his *Many a Green Isle* in 1944, a book about the West Indies. As the publication date approached, the publisher asked Smith to suggest someone noteworthy who could be induced to say something complimentary about the book for publicity's sake. Smith's hopes hinged on two authors: Frances Parkinson Keyes, whom he had met in the Antipodes, and Sinclair Lewis. *Harper's* replied that it would be glad to approach Keyes but didn't dare tackle Lewis and asked if Smith would make the appeal from a personal angle.

Lewis proved not at all intractable and immediately requested that *Harper's* send him proofs. He read the proofs and dashed off an effusive encomium that was printed on an orange ribbon wrapped around the dust jacket when the volume was published.

Shortly thereafter, Lewis dropped in on Smith to congratulate him on the book and to take a look at the large granite plant where the writer worked. Having Sinclair Lewis as a visitor in any office or factory meant a distinct loss in production since workers were quick to observe that they had a celebrity in their midst. Lewis, observing Smith with a fresh sheet of drafting paper on his table, leaned over it with keen interest, and from a fertile imagination described the architectural masterpiece before his eyes while co-workers listened in amazement.

Lewis was always a boon to younger writers, and he did everything he could to assist them. He was interested in the common man, the working class, the man at the Cold Spring Granite Company, or the dentist in St. Cloud. That he always failed to become a part of society was a result of his struggle to create a mystique rather than to try to gain favor. It was more fun to poke fun at society than to be a part of it, especially when his witticisms might determine the direction in which society would be headed.

He always had a passionate regard for children. Nieces Virginia and Isabel Lewis loved their "Uncle Sin" and were always excited when he appeared for a visit. As a man of the world, he felt qualified to lend them his advice and was quick to stand in their behalf during family differences of opinion.

In a letter to Claude Lewis dated June 4, 1933, Harry revealed his delight over the prospects of a visit from Virginia and appealed to her father to permit her to exert her independence:

> We would be delighted to have Virginia come and stay for several days before she starts her trip to Europe. I have just written to Freeman suggesting that he get in touch with her and if possible make arrangements so that he might come up with her.
>
> I agree with you that the trip is extremely short but on the other hand, with Virginia so young, it would make all the difference in the world for her to be going this first time with friends so that she will not be lonely in the strangeness of a foreign land. I think that such a trip with dependable friends

would be worth more than twice as long a trip by herself, on which she might be rather frightened by the differentness of everything.

Claude was accustomed to, but not weary of, Harry's giving advice to his children—especially to Virginia, who was at an age when advice could be most useful. When Virginia deserted St. Cloud for Minneapolis, where she considered pursuing a career, her uncle promptly delivered advice that helped shape her future:

> You, Ginny, can do the same thing [as I have] and move around. You can do it there, go to San Francisco, to New York, to New Orleans, and to Tokyo, and that's all right, or you can do different things and stay right here in Minneapolis. But you can't do both.[27]

Lewis, of course, had shuttled from coast to coast and continent to continent, but never had he found satisfaction. Did he not feel that he had severed his ties with his family, his friends, and the haunts of his

Claude Lewis's home at 724-4th Ave. So. as it looks today. It now serves as the Alumni House of St. Cloud State University. Photograph by Catherine Keller, 1979.

youth? He periodically came home to St. Cloud to be with his family, always within the confines of his own Stearns County, just a stone's throw away from his native Sauk Centre.

In a letter to Virginia Lewis dated December 9, 1945, Lewis epitomized the St. Cloud he was fond of but never could be fully a part of:

> Yes, I would so much like to go to St. Cloud for Christmas but, as I have just written to Isabel and your father, I simply can't make it. I hope you'll have a radiant time, and fish through the ice for gold-fish sixteen feet long, and dance with 6700 young men each handsomer than all the others, and find, as you face the mince pie, that all the laws of limitation of digestion have been suspended for at least one day.

He was an outsider and, like a penniless little boy with his nose pressed against the window of the candy store, he was destined to remain that way.

SINCLAIR LEWIS SITES IN ST. CLOUD

37. Dr. Claude Lewis residence: 710 Fourth Avenue South (razed).
38. Dr. Claude Lewis residence: 724 Fourth Avenue South.
39. Dr. Charles Brigham residence: 426 Third Avenue South (razed).
40. Emily Brigham residence: 424 Third Avenue South (razed).
41. Dr. Claude Lewis clinic: 101 Seventh Avenue South (razed).
42. St. Cloud Country Club: Rural Route 5 (razed).

3

St. Paul

Now we've come out for the winter and spring—possibly next
summer, too—in this middlewestern environment, watching
the solid, stolid Real America in its faults and virtues, its sta-
bility and reluctances. And there is an easy friendliness here
rather pleasant. . . . Also lower rent.[1]

DURING THE SUMMER of 1902, Sinclair Lewis rattled into St. Paul aboard
the fast-flying Flyer to take his entrance examinations for college.[2] He
had previously written Cyrus Northrup, president of the University
of Minnesota, describing his qualifications and preparations and in-
quiring about the feasibility of his plans.

President Northrup, who served in that capacity from 1884 to 1911,
informed Lewis that he required still another year of preparation;
E. J. Lewis firmly agreed, aware that his son's grades were anything
but spectacular. Personnel from the university persuaded Dr. Lewis to
change his mind, however, and Harry was permitted to take his examinations.

The tests were held in the old Capitol High School. E. J. Lewis told
his son to look up an old friend, Bert Hanson, to obtain the twenty-
five dollars needed to pay all of his expenses. Lewis lodged at the
Clarendon Hotel on Sixth and Wabasha streets.

The trip to St. Paul was most rewarding for the young Lewis. Sauk
Centre was a small prairie town, but St. Paul and its neighbor, Minneapolis, were cities on the move, and he welcomed the experience of
visiting them.

Because he was eager to shed his image of a country visitor, he was
quick to show his appreciation for the elegant Victorian mansions that
dotted St. Paul's exclusive Summit Hill.[3] During his exploration of the
city, he roamed the length of fashionable Summit Avenue, from its
stately cathedral at one end to the Mississippi River at the other. On
the "Avenue of the Barons" the city's aristocracy had settled, and

Lewis surveyed the palatial homes of Hill, Forepaugh, Driscoll, Ordway, Burbank, Lindeke, and Griggs.

St. Paul was a booming city for architects, and many of the state's gifted designers resided on the elm-lined avenues on the "hill": E. P. Bassford, Cass Gilbert, Clarence Johnston, and Louis Lockwood on Ashland; Thomas Holyoke on Laurel; J. Walter Stevens on Holly; and George Wirth on Portland.[4] Houses designed by these individuals and others prompted Lewis's interest in materialistic gain, and he would be impressed by palatial estates and their owners throughout his life.

In October 1917, Lewis, his wife, Grace, and their newborn child, Wells, came from New York to spend two weeks on a poultry farm near Marine-on-St. Croix in Minnesota before heading toward Minneapolis in search of a place to live.[5] Lewis was impressed by the rocky, hilly farms that were so reminiscent of his beloved New England.

During the two weeks spent on the farm, the Lewis's St. Paul friends urged them to come and live in St. Paul for the winter; Lewis, remembering his fascination for the Summit Avenue neighborhood, headed directly for that fashionable thoroughfare.[6] With the baby creating added expense, the Lewises felt that St. Paul would be cheaper than New York and would provide background information for the novel *Main Street* (which he had conceived as early as 1905 as "The Village Virus"), and would enlighten them as to what the Twin Cities rivalry was about.

Lewis piloted his new Hupmobile into town, and Grace and the baby followed by train. The Lewises had learned that it was actually cheaper to rent in a good neighborhood than in a poor one, and they rented at 516 Summit Avenue on October 25, 1917. Lewis called it the "lemon meringue pie" house because of its bright yellow brick spotted with dabs of whipped cream marble. It was the scene of many parties to which the hosts invited both wealthy industrialists and Farmer-Labor liberals.

The house served as an excellent place to live, an ideal place for the parties the Lewises were accustomed to giving, and a peaceful retreat for soul searching. It was not, however, a good place in which to write. Initially, Lewis converted a spare bedroom into a study, but too great was the temptation to abandon his writing in favor of a cup of coffee or a relaxing stroll up the elm-lined boulevard.

Lewis sought a workroom elsewhere and discovered several within walking distance. After renting a room, he grew tired of it, and took a series of rooms in dingy rooming houses or servant's quarters, which

Sinclair Lewis house at 516 Summit in St. Paul. Lewis rented this "lemon meringue pie" house on October 25, 1917 and composed his play Hobohemia here. Photograph by Eric Carlson, 1980.

bordered the alleys. The purpose of renting separate workroom was twofold: He required a quiet room away from family and friends where he could accomplish a good day's writing, and he needed the exercise and fresh air he obtained by walking to and from the room everyday. It mattered little what the room looked like, where it was located, or what kind of view the window offered since his mind was geared to writing and nothing else.

Discovering something with substance to write about was his chief concern. *Main Street* was still an abstraction. His chief motivation for returning to St. Paul was to write a book about empire builder James J. Hill. During his earlier visits to St. Paul, he had walked up and down Summit Avenue, scrutinized the Hill house and other citadels like it, and walked away with a compelling desire to write a book. But, though he felt at home in Minnesota and though the Hill house was at his doorstep, he could not write.

James J. Hill was a man who had realized the great American dream: He had started from scratch and conquered the nation with his railroad wealth. In 1856, when only eighteen years old, he left Canada and came to St. Paul to catch the Red River oxcarts for Pembina and Fort Garry.[7] He accepted a position as a steamship clerk and transported cargo on the Red River. Later he launched his own steamboat. After the onset of the Panic of 1873, Hill took over a failing railroad and converted it into the Great Northern; he quickly became one of the wealthiest men in the country.

Lewis was impressed by Hill's rags-to-riches evolution, but he quickly realized that it was not the American dream he wanted to chronicle and not one that the majority of his countrymen could relate to. He longed to write about middle-class Americans who formed the nation's backbone, the working class whose dreams were never realized and seldom chronicled; he abandoned the Hill effort after several abortive attempts to put it down on paper. He was beginning to realize that the book he wanted to write was *Main Street*.

It was, perhaps, at about this time that Lewis launched his "Back to America" literary crusade. He wanted to compose a book about the people's America, heralding its conquests but also laying bare its faults. He felt that for years American authors had been weaving fairy tales. There were no knights in shining armor, he believed, and America's dirty linen must be hung in full view of those who knew it best. If America's story were to be told, Lewis felt he was the man to tell it.

It was neither the Hill novel nor *Main Street* that Lewis wove that summer of 1917, but a bouncy little play entitled *Hobohemia*.[8] Thus commenced a consanguinity with the local Little Theater Association and its twenty-four-year-old producer-director, Danny Reed. Reed had come to St. Paul via Chicago and was best known for his role in *The Time of the Cuckoo*, the final play to be presented at New York's now-demolished Empire Theater. He also was seen in his adaptations from *Spoon River Anthology* with his two children, Susan and Jared. Young Reed assisted Lewis with *Hobohemia*, practically living in the Lewis home. In addition to serious composition, the two found time for skating, skiing, bobsledding, and other popular winter activities.

By January 1918, the team of Lewis and Reed had their play in working order, although it lacked some of the polish Lewis would later give it. That month, a group of society people gathered in the Lewis home to hear Reed narrate *Hobohemia*, which had appeared in the *Saturday Evening Post*, and the event was recorded in the *St. Paul Pioneer Press*:

> A group of society folk will assemble tomorrow evening at the home of Mr. and Mrs. Sinclair Lewis . . . to hear Danny Reed, producing director of the Little Theater Association read the dramatization of Mr. Lewis's play, "Hobohemia," which recently appeared in the Saturday Evening Post.[9]

Little Theatre Association, Ramsey and Pleasant, St. Paul. Lewis worked with the theatre's twenty-four year old producer-director Danny Reed on *Hobohemia*. Photograph by Constance Gunnufson, 1980.

Lewis completed the play on February 9, 1918, and hastily retired to a lumber camp near Cass Lake, Minnesota.[10] His Cass Lake excursion had set his St. Paul neighbors whispering because the camp had recently been the scene of agitation by the Industrial Workers of the World. The Lewises were already under fire because they had refused to discharge "the best nurse in St. Paul" simply because she was German; with the United States at war with Germany, their action was not easily tolerated by St. Paul socialites. St. Paul residents also took a dim view of Lewis's defense of Fritz Kreisler, who had sent home money from his American concerts to assist Austrian artists who were also wounded soldiers.

Lewis was suddenly very unpopular; friends telephoned, demanding his silence before he ended up in prison. It was time to move on, and on March 27, 1918, the Lewises departed from St. Paul. *Hobohemia* fared no better than Lewis did, for when it was presented in the Greenwich Village Theater in New York in 1919, it was panned by the critics.

During the summer of 1922, F. Scott and Zelda Fitzgerald had taken rooms in the fashionable White Bear Yacht Club to the north of St. Paul. The Fitzgeralds, who were partying a great deal that summer, firmly believed that "if you were good enough you not only could live according to the hedonistic code of the Twenties but would probably turn out better for doing so."[11]

Lewis may not have shared these sentiments, but he was among the steady flow of visitors to the Fitzgerald quarters at the yacht club that summer. The older and wiser Lewis and the younger and more optimistic Fitzgerald were of two separate molds, but both were writing about real America, though from different viewpoints. Fitzgerald had recently completed his novel *The Beautiful and Damned* and between parties was at work on a play that he considered his finest work. His writings about America and Americans reflected the tinseled elite, the upper class, that section of America he so heartily wanted to be a part of. Lewis had just published two novels, *Main Street* (1920) and *Babbitt* (1922). He, too, was writing about America, but it was the backbone of the nation, the middle class, that most interested him.

Lewis, though he visited Fitzgerald, had never cared for his writing.[12] Instead, he preferred Ernest Hemingway and, later, John Steinbeck, who could write a masterpiece in a single draft. He was especially fond of playwright Eugene O'Neill and considered playwriting the champagne of literature, regretting that he himself did not possess the necessary tools of a dramatist.[13]

Lewis refused to discuss Fitzgerald or his work publicly, even when pressed, but he did dissect the author with a few close friends. When asked for his opinion of the author of *This Side of Paradise*, he would always shift the conversation to another author, someone like Philip Wylie, whom he considered a cad for abandoning his wife, Eleanor, to move in with the "big electric trains" (as Lewis described Wylie's writer cronies).

Despite Lewis's disdain for Fitzgerald, their visits passed without a ripple. Lewis had always been fond of Minnesota and Minnesotans; he was proud of this native son, who had been causing such a sensation.

Whenever he was in St. Paul, Lewis would drop by Fitzgerald's favorite hangout, the Kilmarnock Bookshop, located in the loop.[14] The Kilmarnock's proprietors, writers Tom and Peggy Boyd, provided interesting conversation. Tom Boyd was the author of a popular novel, *Through the Wheat* (1923), and was the literary editor of the *St. Paul Daily News*.

Many interesting guests, eager for conversation, lounged in the

Boyds' shop. In addition to Fitzgerald, Lewis would chat with, among others, painter Bob Brown, lithographer George Resler, writer Meridel LeSueur, and, when he was in the Twin Cities, gifted wordsmith Joseph Hergesheimer.

In 1939 Lewis returned to St. Paul for a reception given in his honor, and it was there he met Gov. Harold E. Stassen. The governor expressed his appreciation for Lewis's straightforward realism and discovered that the author possessed "a quick, alert, charismatic interest in current events, a probing for human psychological reflections, and a combination of significant and humorous recollections of Minnesota." [15]

Lewis, on the other hand, was quick to congratulate Stassen for his rise from "Main Street." The governor, raised in West St. Paul, was elected at age thirty-one, becoming the state's youngest chief executive. This rapid rise so overwhelmed Lewis that he became a dedicated follower who spearheaded a campaign for Stassen for president.

Initially, it is hard to understand Lewis's interest in Stassen, for the same Lewis had embraced Eugene Debs, founder of the American Socialist Party and controversial labor leader, as perhaps the greatest man who had ever lived. [16] Lewis's esteem for the governor, however, remains curious only if one fails to recognize that he was a believer in the democratic spirit. Like James J. Hill, Stassen had risen from humble beginnings and through his own diligence and hard work had reshaped his destiny. Lewis had always admired those who could rise above the masses, especially when that rise was a result of that leader's own ingenuity. He admired Stassen because he was the local boy who had made good and because Stassen was the champion of the common man.

In St. Paul Lewis was invited to address the Legislature. [17] When he entered the capitol, one legislator mistook him for labor leader John L. Lewis and attempted to bar him from speaking. When the confusion had ended, an angry Lewis launched a full-scale attack on American provincialism.

In 1942 Lewis returned to the Twin Cities and lunched with Stassen at the capitol, attended a performance of the Minneapolis Symphony Orchestra conducted by Sergei Vasilyevich Rachmaninoff, and visited old friends in the offices of the *Minneapolis Tribune*. [18] Lewis had always had close friends in publisher John Cowles and the newspaper's vice president, William McNally. A host of reporters was always glad to see him whenever he came to the Twin Cities.

Lewis had convinced himself that he would like to write a piece about Stassen, and he began extensive research in the archives of the Minnesota Historical Society and the State Capitol. Full of enthusiasm for Stassen, he promised him a big party when both he and the governor would be in New York. In New York Lewis met Governor Stassen at several receptions, one of which was given by Mrs. Ogden Reid of the *New York Herald-Tribune* and was attended by a number of prominent statesmen and journalists.[19]

Returning to St. Paul that same year in search of a teaching position, Lewis freely assisted young writers who displayed a degree of talent. At Hamline University in St. Paul, Lewis delivered a lecture entitled "Environments Don't Make Good Writers." He firmly believed that writers create their own environments.[20]

Lewis's ex-wife, Dorothy Thompson, was in town October 28 to deliver a lecture before eleven thousand people. Another lecturer, F. P. Adams, had spoken in the same hall earlier in the day; St. Paul author Grace Flandrau invited Lewis and the two speakers to her fashionable home on Pleasant Avenue for dinner. Lewis was undoubtedly apprehensive about being thrust into the company of his former wife, especially in full view of others, but accepted the invitation gracefully. The dinner went smoothly; Lewis and Dorothy talked as if there never had been a breach in their relationship, and he attended her lecture that evening. After the speaking engagement, it was Lewis who drove her to the train station.

In September 1947, Lewis made his last pilgrimage to St. Paul in an effort to establish the roots he had lost over a lifetime of loneliness. It was an older, more tired Lewis now—no longer the fast-talking, witty rebel who had once attempted to change the world. He was aware that his writing talent was waning. He once could write only when drinking; now he could no longer write effectively with or without liquor. He had exhausted his themes and was constantly rehashing older ones, trying to mold something from nothing, like a sculptor without clay.

Lewis had come home to write a great novel about Minnesota and the state's founding fathers, the people who had opened the wilderness to civilization. He was absorbed in research for two months in the archives of the Minnesota Historical Society, preparing to write his historical novel, *The God-Seeker*.[21] Resident historian Grace Lee Nute was away at the time, and since her office was not in use, it was turned over to Lewis to use as he saw fit.

Lewis was without doubt intrigued by his Minnesota heritage. In his novel he utilized more than fifty of the state's most famous pioneers, men who had shaped the history of Minnesota. The events in *The*

God-Seeker were in themselves fictitious, as were many of the characters, but the book was based heavily on the Minnesota experience. The authentic pioneers used as characters in the book gave the volume credibility.

The book reads like a who's who in Minnesota history, and if the reader carefully overlooks characters such as Aaron Gadd and the Reverend Balthazar Harge, one discovers the names mentioned in any Minnesota history book: Alexander Ramsey, Henry Sibley, Samuel and Gideon Pond, Harriet Bishop, Henry Rice, Martin McLeod, Little Crow, Bishop Joseph Cretin, Joe Rolette, Norman Kittson, Father Lucien Galtier, Lawrence Taliaferro, and Philander Prescott.

Lewis's protagonist, Aaron Gadd, sought God and Minnesota, but so did the book's author. Gadd became a composite of all the men of the prairie, men who had cast their fears aside and traveled to the frontier in search of their destinies. Gadd may have been a hero, but his creator, Sinclair Lewis, was not. Lewis could only write about heroes, the people he admired most—the Joe Browns and Joe Rolettes, the magic stuff that Aaron Gadd was made of.

The God-Seeker required extensive research but it was, surprisingly, an easy book to write, since Lewis was so familiar with the state's lore; it was, in fact, a labor of love. Now in the twilight of his career, Lewis dreamed, like Gadd, of casting his fears aside, going home to the prairie, and being accepted as at least a minor hero. He desperately wanted to be accepted as part of the Minnesota heritage, a small but worthy chapter in its vast history. Yet he was no fool; whereas Gadd had found a home in Minnesota, Lewis realized that he could not. It was much too late.

Despite his dedication to the novel, Lewis took time to coach young, aspiring writers who were temporarily in St. Paul.[22] Ann Chidester, a Stillwater writer, and Frederick Manfred and his wife visited Lewis in his rooms in the Hotel St. Paul. The Manfreds and Miss Chidester recently had called upon Lewis in Duluth and, despite their youthfulness, were considered old friends to whom he would give advice. No one could know it, but they were paying their last farewell to the mentor who was quitting St. Paul for good.

Another young writer whom Lewis attracted was James Roers, who was working on a master's in American civilization at the University of Minnesota.[23] Lewis hired Roers as a research assistant and dispatched him to read up on pioneer lifestyles for *The God-Seeker*. Roers served as a walking reference text, and for $250 per month plus room, board, and chess, was required to give the correct answer when Lewis might inquire what kind of dress Mrs. Ramsey might have worn for a special occasion or what kind of gun Henry Sibley might have taken squirrel hunting.

On November 12, 1947, Lewis left St. Paul and Minnesota for good, taking research assistant Roers with him to Thorvale Farm in Williamstown, Massachusetts. Minnesota, Massachusetts, New York— they were all mere stopping places, watering holes to temporarily satisfy him on the voyage he had made all his life. Roers was plucked from the Twin Cities as others were speared from nearly every place he lived, for Lewis feared to live alone. Solitude was required for writing, but once the typewriter ceased, someone—a friend, a research assistant, a wife—had to be present to give him the conversation he required to combat loneliness.

Writer Betty Stevens Alexander recalls one conversation with Lewis:

> Before I went up to my room he briefed me on the protocol of Thorvale Farm, in much the same way, I gathered, as he had all his other visitors. "I'm on a tight schedule up here," he began, "I get up very early and write until noon. Sometimes I stop about eleven and take a walk before lunch. But I'll see you at lunchtime. I take a nap every afternoon and write a few more hours. So, sleep late if you like, read anything you want. Or prowl around the grounds. Make yourself at home. There's a swimming pool over there. Do anything you like, Child. This is your vacation."[24]

SINCLAIR LEWIS SITES IN ST. PAUL

43. Sinclair Lewis residence: 516 Summit Avenue.
44. Little Theater Association: Corner of Ramsey Street and Pleasant Avenue.
45. Grace Flandrau residence: 385 Pleasant Avenue (razed).
46. Clarendon Hotel: Northeast corner of Wabasha and Fifth streets (razed).
47. White Bear Yacht Club: 56 Dellwood Avenue, Dellwood, White Bear Lake.
48. Gov. Harold E. Stassen residence: 744 Stewart Lane, South St. Paul.
49. Hamline University: Hewitt and Snelling avenues.
50. Minnesota State Capitol: University Avenue and Robert Street.
51. Minnesota Historical Society: 690 Cedar Street.
52. Hotel St. Paul (Sinclair Lewis): 363 St. Peter Street.

4

Cass Lake

When old Paul Bunyan died at last
He left his ox, his hoss,
His round turns and his lepercauns [sic]
To Cousin Johnny Goss.

John was a man weighed ninety stone
He ate at every meal,
Four German counts, two tons of snuff,
And half a paddle wheel.

His tempers were so terrible
That he and Foreman Harmon
Would beat up each sweet lumberjack
That they could get an arm on.

They caught poor Lester Stewart once
Attending Sunday School,
And beat the poor boy's ears half off
With a U.S. scaling rule.

When John and Harmon found no one
To bite or choke or smother,
These friends would lock the wanigan
And nearly kill each other.

From Ball Club to Bemidji folks
Would hide beneath their beds
When they saw John and Robert roll
Off drunken from their sleds.

Till folks could stand these two no more,
And gave them to the jailer,
And in their place elected youths
Named Higginski and Taylor.

The world may not have heard the truth,
But these sad facts are,
That Higginski was secretly
The late lamented Czar.

If John and Robert really were
Most criminally bad
For fierce and fearsome naughtiness
They could not touch this lad.

He frightened teamsters and cookess [sic]
And other timber friskers
By shaking his deep purple, long,
And badly tangled whiskers.

He wore a wolf's head on one arm,
A diamond on his hand
And oh his voice it sounded like
The Bena City Band.

As bad as he, and worse in spots,
Was Taylor, his side kick,
Who nineteen swampers between nine
and nine fifteen would lick.

They say this Taylor traveled once
Before a minstrel show
But when the show caught up with him,
Of course he had to go.

Well underneath these hounds of hell,
Was Clarence Merry, cook,
I liked him . . . till once in the beans
I found a top chain hook.

And once a log wrench in the cake,
And once, alas, alack,
Among the spuds I sadly found
A toasted lumberjack.

Now why should honest woodsmen stand
For vicious men like those.
I have a decent gentleman
As camp boss to propose.

Red Michel's hair it looks like mine,

His whiskers even more so.
Let's make him boss at Lake Thirteen,
Our troubles will be o'er so.

You've noticed, if you've traveled much,
By foot or train or sled,
That all good honest able men
Are always, ALWAYS red.[1]

UPON COMPLETION of his play *Hobohemia* in St. Paul in February 1918, Lewis traveled alone to a lumber camp in Cass Lake, Minnesota, to experience the great north woods in winter.[2] The camp had been the scene of recent IWW agitation, and Lewis, already unpopular in St. Paul for refusing to discharge a German nurse in wartime and for his defense of Kreisler's sending money to Austrian artists, did little to enhance his reputation with St. Paul citizens.[3]

For Lewis, his trip was a delightful respite following the arduous labors involved with *Hobohemia*. He planned no writing in Cass Lake but intended only to observe the American worker. Logging operations had changed little since the inception of the industry in the nineteenth century.

Cass Lake and Cass County were named for Gen. Lewis Cass, governor of the Michigan Territory, who led an expedition into the Minnesota wilderness in 1820 in search of the source of the Mississippi River.[4] The Great Northern Railway established the first railroad in this section of the country in 1898, which was a contributing factor, if not the primary factor, in the establishment of the town of Cass Lake. The village was incorporated in 1899, the United States Government Land Office initiated in 1903, and the first school organized in 1904.

Lumbering was the primary industry in the early days of the settlement. Conservation became a national issue under the Theodore Roosevelt administration, and the Cass Lake region was designated as a national park, although later it became part of the Chippewa National Forest.

Cass Lake, 1,367 feet above sea level, lies at the western entrance of the Chippewa National Forest, which abounds in lakes, rivers, and heavy stands of pine. The area's economy is largely dependent on two natural resources, its woods and its lakes.

Lewis worked at the camp of Judson M. Goss, located on the south shore of Bear Lake (later called Partridge Lake) in an area called Pike Bay.[5] The Goss family had been active in the lumber industry for years and operated several camps near Cass Lake.

Lewis's foreman was red-haired John Michel, whose auburn locks were characteristic enough of the Lewis family to make him an "honorary" Lewis. Lewis enjoyed working under Michel, who exhibited an immediate affinity toward him, and the pair became close friends over the five-day span. Red Michel told Lewis what the north-woods winter experience was really like. No one possessed a keener knowledge of lumbering in the Cass Lake-Chippewa area than did Michel, and he proved an able teacher.

In the lumber camp, Lewis met a variety of fellow workers: timber cruisers, who selected areas to be cut, designated sites for future camps, and determined the most suitable routes for tote roads and navigable water routes to carry the logs; and choppers, swampers, and barkers, who cut trees, stripped branches, and slashed bark from the underside of each tree to make skidding logs a simpler task.[6]

Each camp consisted of a concentration of primitive buildings, including a "shanty" with a hole in the roof to permit smoke to escape; a "wanigan," or store; a bunkhouse that often housed as many as eighty lumberjacks; and the cookhouse, where the cook and his assistant, the cookee, prepared flapjacks, pork and beans, molasses, biscuits, and meat and potatoes. Lights were extinguished at nine o'clock every evening, and those who elected not to sleep would smoke a pipe, chew

Lewis traveled alone to a lumber camp in Cass Lake, Minnesota to "experience the great north woods in winter." He penned a lengthy ballad recording his adventure. Photograph courtesy Stanley Johnson, Director Cass County Historical Society.

tobacco or snuff, tell stories, sing folk ballads, or dance to the music of fiddles and accordions.

Liquor was not permitted in the camps, but when the lumberjacks received their pay, many of them would wander into town and raise hell along the skid roads, but the carousing of the lumberjack frequently has been exaggerated.

Lumberjacks relished singing, dancing, and the laughter that accompanied it, and every day there were new songs composed about life in the camps. The lumberjacks were a hard-working lot and there was little time for play, but they made the most of the free time allotted them. Lewis enjoyed being cast amid these professional storytellers, whose tall tales, whopping lies, and campfire chats, related in the land where Paul Bunyan and Babe the Blue Ox stalked, combined atmosphere with fiction. There were stories about each man in the camp, and Lewis was delighted to be one of the gang.

What impressed Lewis most about the logging camp was the camaraderie of the working men. They may have had their differences, and it was common to find two men fighting, but on the job they became a single driving force. Their leaders, men like Goss and Michel, were never monarchs, but were members of the gang. They kept their men in line, and their word was never doubted, and every lumberjack respected them.

Lewis, as an outsider, was continuing his search for the real America in a northern Minnesota lumber camp. *Main Street* was already germinating in his head, and his desire to present America just as he found it was uppermost in his mind. His observations in a primitive north-woods community afforded him a prime example of American realism—not the picture of lumber barons or oil magnates that most American authors portrayed, but that of the average worker, whose hard work helped to shape America.

One of Lewis's lifelong ambitions was to write a great labor novel depicting the struggles of the working class; the experience at Cass Lake may have been the catalyst. The IWW and the Nonpartisan League were struggling to organize the workers, and the former was still active in the logging camps of northern Minnesota.

If his logging experience provided the roots for the great labor novel he would never write, it may also have been a prerequisite for *The God-Seeker*, the novel he did write thirty years later. In the camp environment of Cass Lake, Lewis was in the company of men like Aaron Gadd, the novel's protagonist, men who were not deterred by hardship or defeat.

When Lewis departed from Cass Lake after only five days, he left behind a coterie of real friends. He penned a light-hearted poem recounting his north-woods experience, the narrative of which included all his lumber cronies. (The poem begins this chapter.) Lewis gave copies of the poem to each family represented in it, emphasizing that it had been written in jest and not for any lasting literary value.

There was nothing unique about Lewis's folklore ballad; scores of them were written every day. Depicting life in the camps, they bore such curious titles as "Ole from Norway," "The Crow Wing Drive," "Ye Noble Big Pine Tree," "The Festive Lumber-Jack," "Jim Whalen," "The Merry Shanty Boys," "Bung Yer Eye," and "The Three McFarlands."[7] A complete volume, *Ballads and Songs of the Shanty-Boy*, appeared in 1926.

The final two lines of Lewis's ballad, "That all good honest able men / Are always, ALWAYS red," could have had several implications: the color of hair, a raw-skinned complexion, or political preference. Lewis attended meetings of the Nonpartisan League a year after his stay at Cass Lake, but he became affiliated with no political party (the sole exception being the 1939 Republican presidential campaign of Harold E. Stassen). His reference to the "good honest able men" simply signified the working class.

Sinclair Lewis left Cass Lake as he had found it, and in this rustic land of Paul Bunyan, a new legacy of tall tales was ready to be told.

SINCLAIR LEWIS SITE IN CASS LAKE

53. Goss Logging Camp: South shore of Bear Lake on Pike Bay.

5

Minneapolis

At first sight, Minneapolis is so ugly. Parking lots like scabs. Most buildings are narrow, drab, dirty, flimsy, irregular in relationship to one another—a set of bad teeth. Window frames either bleak or vice versa, over ornamented. But modern Star-Journal-Tribune and Farmers and Mechanics Bank, gray stone and sleek, yet strong, seem suited to a modern city as Minneapolis should be.[1]

IN JANUARY 1904, eighteen-year-old Sinclair Lewis discovered prominent poet Arthur Wheelock Upson living in Minneapolis.[2] Lewis had initially learned of Upson in Jessie B. Rittenhouse's *Younger American Poets* and was determined to meet him. He timorously wrote Upson a letter and was surprised to receive a warm reply from the author. Seven or eight letters soon were exchanged, after which Lewis spent "four glorious days" with Upson in Minneapolis.

Upson was the author of four volumes of poetry: *At the Sign of the Harp* (1900), *Poems* (1902), *Octaves in an Oxford Garden* (1902), and *The West Wind Songs* (1902). He was heralded as a bright young American poet. A fifth volume, *The City: A Poem Drama*, was published in 1904.

Lewis visited Upson in Minneapolis regularly from 1904 to 1908. In Upson, he found someone he could admire and hope to emulate. With the poet, he could discuss literature, something he hadn't been able to do since Irving Fisher moved from Sauk Centre. But Fisher had never been a writer and had never borne the struggle that tears within any young writer's breast. He could appreciate fine literature but could not create it. Upson could and did, and he was only too eager to share his talent with Lewis.

In August 1908, Lewis's world was thrown into chaos when Upson's boat capsized in Lake Bemidji and the author drowned. "Adonais is dead," Lewis wrote in an article mourning the death of his mentor and friend. Lewis felt a Keats had been snuffed out in youth, and

53

although most Americans could hardly mourn for a man they had hardly known, Lewis was crushed.

With Upson's passing, Lewis's visits to Minneapolis were less frequent. After spending the winter of 1917–18 in St. Paul, Lewis, his wife, Grace, and their infant son, Wells, returned to Minneapolis on October 21, 1918, and occupied a house at 1801 James Avenue South.³

Lewis rented a bare office on Harmon Place in the Loring Park district of the city and went to work on his novel *Free Air*, as well as another, soon entitled "For Sale Cheap." *Free Air* had already been accepted by publisher Alfred Harcourt for serialization, but the other novel was rejected. Harcourt urged Lewis to devote more time to *Free Air* and to abandon the other project altogether. "For Sale Cheap" had already been rejected by *Everybody's, Cosmopolitan, Hearst's, Red Book*, and other publications, and Lewis finally shelved the book to devote all his time to the better novel.

Harcourt also urged him to write the book he wanted to write and to forget about writing the kind of book he felt the public wanted. This was probably easy for Lewis to do since Harcourt had already accepted the novel in rough draft, and he was not forced to write for any particular market.

Sinclair Lewis home at 1801 James Avenue South, Minneapolis. Lewis rented the house on October 21, 1918 and worked on his novel Free Air here. Photograph Constance Gunnufson, 1980.

But despite Harcourt's plea, Lewis felt he was writing *Free Air* for money, and he continued to struggle with the expanded version. But even though he was preoccupied with *Free Air*, he already contemplated another book about people, institutions and lifestyles—a novel to be called *Main Street*.

The Minneapolis experience was good for both *Free Air* and *Main Street*. Lewis was writing about the Midwest, and it was only fitting that he be familiar with the territory he was chronicling. The previous year, he and his wife had enjoyed St. Paul and had experienced a warm feeling of acceptance until some of their activities aroused suspicion. Security, roots, belonging—he had them all in Minneapolis.

The author lectured at the Minneapolis Institute of Arts on "Contemporary Fiction as an Interpretation of Modern Life" but also found time to party at the home of Joseph Warren Beach, head of the English department at the University of Minnesota.

The Beaches were well known for their parties and always had numerous literary celebrities on hand when they entertained. Liquor flowed freely, and Lewis, who drank his share, became well known for his sharp tongue. Many Midwesterners were not prepared for his humor, and Lewis often caused embarrassing rows.

At one dinner party given by the Beaches, Lewis arrived toting a bottle of whiskey. He draped a towel over his shoulder to imitate a waiter and began serving liquor to the guests. His impersonations were humorous to some, but others did not take the experience lightly.

On another occasion, Mrs. Lewis complained about the way he ate his peas. Sulking, Lewis jerked his plate from the table and sat down on the floor in a corner, continuing to eat his peas in his own style.

Lewis devoted most of his time to the empty office and *Free Air*, but he continued to grapple with the plot to *Main Street*. Overwhelmed by a multiplicity of plot devices, he was still observing, still collecting data, but was not ready to put those ideas onto paper.

The title *Main Street* had existed since 1905, although Lewis was initially reluctant to scrap his original title, "The Village Virus." *Main Street* had such a simple, literary ring that he wondered why no one had used it before.

In an early draft, Lewis had referred to his novel as "The Village Virus" because it chronicled his resentment toward the moral fiber of a small town, depicting how each resident became a prisoner of society, languishing under the microscope of one's neighbors. At this stage, a young lawyer, Guy Pollack, not Carol Kennicott, was the central character. Carol, who is described as "tall, weedy and incurably rakish," more closely resembled Sinclair Lewis than Pollack did.

Vida Sherwin, the teacher in *Main Street*, was inspired by Stella Louise Wood, whose Kindergarten Primary Training School had a national reputation for excellence. When the young mothers of Minneapolis decided that there should be a public kindergarten, Miss Wood was summoned from Dubuque, Iowa, even before the Minneapolis Board of Education approved the action. With Wells nearing two years of age, Mrs. Lewis was among these enthusiastic mothers, and she and Miss Wood became close friends over the years. Lewis was so fascinated with this woman that he could not resist using her as a character.

In Minneapolis, as in St. Paul, the Lewises soon aroused the suspicion of their friends and neighbors.[4] They were seen attending a meeting of the Nonpartisan League and later at a lecture delivered by Louise Bryant, widow of Harvard Bolshevist John Reed. And, as always, readers who had enjoyed any association with the author recognized themselves in his stories and became agitated.

It was time to move on, time to continue the cycle of being welcomed and then run out of town. When their lease expired May 1, the Lewises planned to move to the small Minnesota community of Fergus Falls, where the author could give substance to *Main Street* at long last. But when they traveled to the village to secure accommodations, no house could be procured. Instead, they stayed at the Hotel Maryland in Minneapolis until the end of May, when their lease was ready on a house in Mankato.

Twenty years later, on January 17 and 18, 1939, Lewis's play *Angela Is Twenty-Two* opened in St. Paul. It played in Minneapolis January 19, 20, and 21. Lewis's friend, Marcella Powers, played the leading role of Angela. Lewis himself appeared as the fifty-two-year-old Dr. Jarrett, who marries Angela. They performed before a packed house, including two hundred people who had come from Sauk Centre. If anyone in that village was embittered by the *Main Street* controversy, it certainly was not evident in this tribute to their native son.

After the performance, there was a dinner party attended by Gov. Harold E. Stassen and several authors. Delighted to be home in Minneapolis, Lewis remarked that it wasn't so much a homecoming as the case of a person who had gone away, gained a degree of notoriety, and then come back to the place where he had belonged all the time.

In September 1940, he returned to the city again, this time seeking a teaching position at the University of Minnesota.[5] He was undoubtedly the state's most successful author, and that included some stiff competition from F. Scott Fitzgerald. Lewis was convinced he had the necessary credentials to conduct a writing class.

But the size of Minneapolis bothered him, and he decided it wasn't quite what he was looking for. He remembered his unpleasant experience in 1919; he had lost his desire to relocate there, for Minneapolis simply didn't feel like home to him. Instead he chose Madison in nearby Wisconsin and accepted employment as an instructor at the University of Wisconsin.

Lewis's longings for Minnesota, however, brought him back to Minneapolis in January 1942, when he again sought a teaching position.[6] The size of the city and the inhabitants who once bored him no longer bothered him, and he felt a deep need to come home. He remained in the city for ten days, taking over a story-writing class for three two-hour sessions at the University of Minnesota; the sessions impressed him so much that he considered full-time activity at the university. Lewis liked the Minnesota faculty better than the Wisconsin professors, whose knowledge he considered more limited. Brother Claude came down from St. Cloud and they spent a day together, with Harry serving as tour guide.

That spring Lewis rented a spacious home near Excelsior on Lake Minnetonka, preferring to live like a rustic than to take a home in the bustling city. Yet he spent most of his time in the city, visiting old friends and lecturing before filled auditoriums. One of these sessions was before a women's literary society at the University of Minnesota, where he delivered a lecture entitled "Stay West, Young Woman."

Having spent the spring and summer in Excelsior, Lewis was eager to find a house in the city for the winter. He had been working on his novel *Gideon Planish*, and the time was ripe for securing a teaching position at the University of Minnesota.

Most houses at Lewis's disposal were in the fashionable Lowry Hill-Kenwood area. He jested considerably about the monstrous Victorian houses that had been constructed by self-made millionaires who had amassed fortunes from railroads and tractors. One building, known simply as the Harris house, interested him greatly, but it was no longer available. Another, the Frederick Wheeler house, was available. He toured the residence and nearly rented it, but since it was not quite what he wanted, he resolved he would take it only if he couldn't find something he preferred.

On September 22, 1942, he rented an elegant abode at 1500 Mount Curve Avenue, high atop Lowry Hill. Things finally were going in his favor, for he had landed a teaching position at the University of Minnesota and would be reunited with old friends like Joseph Warren Beach.[7] In room 301 of Folwell Hall, he delivered informal talks to his students, telling them they should submit their three best works.

Sinclair Lewis home at 1500 Mt. Curve in Minneapolis. Lewis rented the home September 22, 1942 and worked on his novel Gideon Planish here. Photograph by Constance Gunnufson, 1980.

He offered to read some pieces aloud and comment on them but promised to avoid embarrassment by not revealing the authors' identities.

Lewis relished working with young, promising writers. He seldom said the things they wanted him to say or even what they expected him to say, but he did teach them how to write. He offered his students the following advice:

> Colleges are full of idiots, but you'd run into the same proportion of idiots if you spent four years elsewhere. . . . Newspaper work may help for awhile, but if you stay in it so long you can't operate unless under assignment, you may find it impossible to write when there's no one but yourself giving orders. Editing a magazine is the worst preparation of all. It would be far better to work in a cobbler's shop. . . . The slick, nimble tricks of the magazine story will ruin you. It's fictional vaudeville, nothing more.[8]

Although realizing he was no longer fashionable—the battles Lewis had waged had already been won or lost—he felt comfortable addressing his students. He was happy to be home in Minnesota, not as a casual visitor but as a genuine resident, and he hoped he could help its native sons.

In June, two months after he had found a "permanent" home in Minneapolis, he remarked to an audience: "A man has to return to his home state sometime. I have long wanted to come back to Minnesota. After all, that's where my heart is."[9]

He advised not only his students but also members of his family.[10] He delighted in counseling his nieces, Virginia and Isabel. If not for Lewis, his nephew Freeman would never have attended Exeter and Harvard but would have enrolled at the University of Minnesota or Carleton College in Northfield. Lewis was very precise in what he wanted them to do with their lives and actively coached his brother Claude in making the correct family decisions.

Lewis's statement that "colleges are full of idiots" was a conviction he firmly believed. In a letter to Virginia Lewis dated February 17, 1933, he echoed some of these same sentiments:

> No, I think your mother is mistaken in saying that I regard it as necessarily wrong to leave the University and use the same money in travelling. However, that is something which must be decided in each individual case. Personally, I don't think a great deal of universities, but then, on the other hand, travel can be a complete waste. The idea that wandering from place to place is necessarily educative is wrong. It has to be a choice which applies differently to different people. Certainly I do not think that it would be an error to drop out of the university for a year and see something of the pageant of life, and then perhaps go back. But I certainly do not want to intrude on this distinctively family problem of yours. I can only say that, as for myself, I have had indefinitely more from travel than from university education.

Every Sunday from five o'clock in the afternoon until two o'clock in the morning, rather than from two until five o'clock in the afternoon, students were permitted to enter his spacious Mount Curve home for a session in his study, where he commented on their work.[11] Joseph Hardrick, the butler, would graciously admit the students and serve cookies and ginger ale while they waited for their turn to enter the study. These sessions frequently were little more than social encounters; girls vying for his attention would huddle on one side of the room and the boys on the other.

Sinclair Lewis was far from being the sole celebrated figure on campus, for novelist Robert Penn Warren, who would gain recognition for *At Heaven's Gate* (1943) and *All the King's Men* (1946), came there to teach the same year and remained for eight years.[12] Lewis was introduced to Warren at a faculty tea and felt extremely uncomfortable in his company, for Warren was a good friend of Allen Tate and John Peale Bishop, both of whom, Lewis had decided, disliked him.

Warren had published three books before coming to Minnesota—*John Brown: Making of a Martyr* (1929), *Thirty-Six Poems* (1935), and *Night Rider* (1939)—and was the recipient of as many awards: the Houghton Mifflin Fellowship (1936), Guggenheim Fellowship (1939), and the Shelley Memorial Award (1942). He represented a new breed of writers and was popular with the students. Lewis did his best to avoid Warren, but the two often were brought together at parties and faculty teas.

Lewis enjoyed compatible relationships with some members of the faculty, especially poetry expert Ione Jackson and his old friend Joseph Warren Beach, but he experienced difficulties with others like Dr. Anna Augusta Von Helmholtz Phelan.[13] Dr. Phelan represented the "old school," an even older school than Lewis's. In attempting to teach her students how to write, she allowed her fondness for the pre-Raphaelites to dictate class direction. The encounter between Lewis and Dr. Phelan was a clash of generations.

What especially bothered Lewis about Dr. Phelan is that she taught the writing seminars he wanted to teach. Despite this frustration, he was sincere in his efforts to get along with her.

The break finally occurred at one of Beach's parties.[14] Dr. Phelan, favoring a heavily bandaged left thumb, was chatting with guests, and Lewis, armed with a drink and a cigarette, sauntered over and inquired about the taped appendage. Dr. Phelan quickly explained that she kept a house full of cats and that, in bathing them, the largest, Nikkipoo, had bitten her through the thumbnail. Lewis, never one to rely on tact, shot back, "Yeah? Why don't you drown the sonofabitch?"

Dr. Phelan was speechless, and so was everyone else nearby. Only Beach laughed; as head of the English department, he could get away with it.

Everyone admired Beach, and famous writers from all parts of the country attended his parties.[15] It was not uncommon to find Meridel LeSueur, Carl Sandburg, or Robert Penn Warren casually chatting with guests. Beach was scholarly, an expert on fiction, an excellent tennis player, and an authority on Henry James, about whom he had written a book that many experts considered the first serious critical analysis of that author.

Like Lewis, Beach relished the matching of opposites. He liked to study the often catastrophic results of his scheming. He always referred to this matching, or mismatching, as "dueling with experts." Though always present when the fun began, he usually remained a spectator. His knack for causing natural enemies to spar resulted in a confrontation between Lewis and James Gray, a St. Paul critic. Gray never had been fond of Lewis's fiction, nor had Lewis ever cared for Gray's comments in the newspapers. The two became embroiled in an argument over Henry James as Beach, the genuine Henry James authority, looked on without comment. The duel was brief; Lewis verbally squashed his opponent.

Angry because he had been embarrassed in front of a group of important people, Gray brought up the subject of Lewis's relationship with a young woman who had a separate room at the Nicollet Hotel. "Why did you leave your girl friend sitting at the Nicollet Hotel, Red?" he taunted. Lewis dashed to the telephone, called the woman, and asked her to come right over. She did.

At another Beach party, a young, cocky Max Shulman was discussing writing with Lewis.[16] Shulman, who was eager to become a good writer, asked, "Mr. Lewis, can you tell me how you make money writing?" "No!" Lewis snapped. "If you want to make money, why don't you open a grocery store?"

Lewis devoted much of his time to the Beaches, but his closest friends in Minneapolis were John and Mary Baxter, the neighbors who resided at 1779 Girard Avenue South.[17] The Baxters gave many parties and always included Lewis in their festivities, regardless of the occasion. Lewis referred to John Baxter as "the Fire Warden" because he served as a volunteer warden during the war years.[18] The Baxters considered Lewis a very lonely man who possessed few loyal friends but who deeply cherished those he did have. Lewis, they realized, was inordinately afraid of being written out and washed up. He had produced nothing of importance in recent years; since the publication of *It Can't Happen Here* (1935), he had written but two novels, *Prodigal Parents* (1938) and *Bethel Merriday* (1940), neither of which had been particularly successful.

Lewis was fond of John Baxter's sister, Helen, who always attended her brother's social gatherings and painted pastels for the various guests.[19] Lewis considered her to be a talented young woman and urged her perseverance in the arts.

Lewis Daniel, a cousin of John and Helen Baxter, was also close to the author. Daniel and his wife, Hanna, frequently attended the parties.

After Lewis had left Minneapolis, he visited the Baxters and the

Daniels whenever he returned to the city, for they numbered among the few loyal friends he had. In a letter to Mary Baxter dated October 23, 1945, Lewis revealed his fondness for her family:

> I hope to have about a week in Minneapolis when going south and expect to see the Baxters daily from 9 A.M. to 6 P.M. for eating, then 6 P.M. to 3 A.M. for chess, local scandal and sandwiches.[20]

He continued to correspond with Mary Baxter through 1947. He wrote to the Daniels as well and dispatched a comforting letter to Hanna January 4, 1944, after the death of her husband.

Perhaps the most interesting group of friends that Lewis inherited in Minneapolis was a clique that called itself Linden Hills White Trash.[21] The group consisted of local writers, artists, and novices, all of whom lived near Lake Harriet and Lake Calhoun. The group boasted a culture all its own, and although it frequently invaded parties with Lewis, it was never part of the elite class.

The group was formed by writer Brenda Ueland, a talented young woman with a formidable disdain for what she termed the "regrettable herd instinct." Miss Ueland had met Lewis in Excelsior earlier in 1942, and when he encouraged her to organize a theater and demanded that she play the part of Hedda Gabbler, they became good friends. Brenda soon invited him to meet the other members of Linden Hills White Trash.

Members of the group included Brenda's three brothers, Arnulf, president of the Midland National Bank and Trust Company, and Rolf and Sigurd, both attorneys; attorney David Shearer and his wife, Henrietta; David's brother, Alan M. Shearer, a writer; artist Barbara Bell; Donald B. Simmons, an employee of the Bemis Bag Company in Wayzata, and his wife, Katherine; Kate MacKinnon Wood; and Glen and Helen Allison.

Every Saturday night the group would assemble for a picnic. With the war raging in Europe and Asia, times were hard and rationing was in effect, but everyone brought something they felt they could spare. Someone in the group would volunteer, or be volunteered, to pose, while those with artistic talent would paint.

It was a congenial group, and members freely discussed any and all subjects. Though Lewis rarely mentioned his ex-wives, Grace Hegger and Dorothy Thompson, he always felt comfortable with this group and often jested about Dorothy, calling her "the talking woman." He said he did not desert Dorothy Thompson but was, in fact, a refugee.

The group frequently gave parties to which both Sinclair Lewis and

Marcella Powers, a frequent companion, were invited. Lewis was always the highlight of these parties with his madcap impersonations, and no one ever was offended by his antics. A most capable mimic, his favorite impersonation was that of "The Martyr." Lewis would be led into the room where all the other guests were seated and was slowly dragged toward the fireplace. Someone would quickly block his path and ask, "Do you retract?" "Certainly not!" was Lewis's predictable reply. He and his captor would proceed closer to the fire; again he would be asked for a retraction, whereupon he again would respond negatively and be led closer to the blaze. The same exchange would be enacted several times, and at last the martyr would "fry." Lewis performed the role well, and his comical mimicking kept the onlookers in stitches, especially Kate Wood, who went into hysterics because of the mimic's orange tweed suit.

The parties frequently were held in Lewis's Mount Curve residence. At home, he played the lordly monarch, but his pride was always hurt if guests failed to return to his parties.

When he wasn't working, Lewis devoted much of his time to old friends who were members of the Minneapolis social set: the William McNallys, the John Cowles, the Pillsburys, the F. Peavey Heffelfin-

John Cowles Residence, 2318 Park Avenue South, Minneapolis. The wealthy publisher was for a time a good friend of Sinclair's. Photograph by Constance Gunnufson, 1980.

gers, the Addison Lewises, Alfred and Fefa Wilson, Harold W. Sweatt, John and Berniece Dalrymple, Hugh and Kate (MacKinnon) Wood, the Rufus Rands, and John and Dorothy (Atkinson) Rood. There were parties and dinners, some hosted by Lewis, others by various members of the elite coterie.

The sprawling Addison Lewis mansion on Long Lake, with its riding track and thoroughbred horses, was a favorite hangout. Various people assembled at the house, the hub of the Minneapolis elite as well as Brenda Ueland and her Linden Hills White Trash, enabling Harry to enjoy the best of both worlds. The white clapboard house overlooking the lake was well known for its opulence, and its owner, an advertising executive, had written two or three fine plays that had been produced locally, one of them at the Old Log Theater in Excelsior. Addison's dream was to have one of his plays produced on Broadway, but his wish was never fulfilled. Addison Lewis and Sinclair Lewis were not related, but they jested over being cousins and remained very good friends.

The John Dalrymples, who topped the hierarchy of Minneapolis social circles during the 1940s, took a shine to the brash author from Sauk Centre.[22] They had been close to F. Scott Fitzgerald and had known him from the 1930s until his death in 1940, but somehow they had failed to bring the two authors together.

Whether visiting or at home, Lewis was constantly in the company of Marcella Powers. Lewis always felt he was being called upon to perform, and mimicked Sauk Centre residents for their rigid customs, something the Dalrymples and their friends didn't find particularly funny. The Dalrymples considered Lewis to be anything but a revolutionary, but he tried to come on that way; at the same time, however, he craved conformity—the "regrettable herd instinct"—and strained to be an accepted part of the social mainstream.

Lewis had an eye for younger women and considered himself quite a ladies' man. This sometimes angered John Dalrymple (or "Handsome Jack" as his intimates called him) and other members of the exclusive fraternity.

Lewis became progressively more unpopular as the year 1942 waned. Antics that once were considered cute now had become antagonizing to many of his confreres, and his continued associations with local radicals ultimately caused the elite to reject him. There was no reason to remain; Marcella had gone East to New York and he was anxious to follow.

He met his last class December 9, 1942, and, with tears in his eyes, departed for New York, which he now called home.[23] He considered

Minneapolis provincial and wanted to tell its citizens that; he felt he no longer had close friends to whom he could relate. There were still the Baxters, the Daniels, the Uelands, and a few others, but he never realized the depth of their loyalty. His admission into social circles had been a disaster, for he had lost friends faster than he could count them. He had mingled with both rich and poor, been wooed by both conservative and radical, some with opinions, others with none. His love affair with the "railroad and tractor" millionaires had ended in bitter disappointment and hadn't measured up to what he thought it would be. He had grown impatient; even the radicals bored him with their endless tirades and banner waving. He had once departed from New York because it had never seemed like home, when Minneapolis appeared to answer his need. Now the situation was reversed, and New York cried "home" once again. His homes had in fact become nothing more than one plush hotel after another.

Between 1943 and 1947, Lewis passed through Minneapolis many times. He always kept in touch with the Baxters and made every effort to see them. In a letter to Mary Baxter dated December 13, 1945, he asked her to find him a suitable hotel because he was tired of imposing on them. His attitude suggested he was weary of Minneapolis and its hostelries, especially those hotels that were considered fashionable: "It would presumably be some place quieter than the Nicollet, Radisson or Dyckman."[24]

On December 22, nine days later, he checked into the Leamington after Mary Baxter had made the necessary arrangements.

Lewis continually boasted of his knowledge of Minnesota lore and found great delight in showing off his familiarity with names, dates, and places. Lewis was so proud of Minnesota that he expected every Minnesotan to know key geographical and historical data by heart. When they professed no knowledge of a certain item, he insulted his guests. When Claude's daughter Isabel and her husband, Robert Agrell, came to Minneapolis, Lewis invited them to dine with him at the Leamington.[25] Lewis, waxing a bit arrogant, asked Bob if he knew who Joseph Renshaw Brown was. Bob said no. "You're from Minnesota," Lewis snapped. Agrell quipped, "I was born and raised in this briar patch." "You don't know who Joseph Renshaw Brown was," the author barked, "You're a fine example of a Minnesotan."

Lewis was back in Minneapolis for a party in 1947.[26] When he arrived, it was apparent to the shocked guests that this was no longer the dashing, word-spitting challenger they had been up against only five years before. His face seemed noticeably pained, and Meridel LeSueur, catching a glimpse of him, broke down in tears. Lewis confided to Meridel that he had lost every woman he had ever loved, and that he had made the mistake of educating his women and transforming them into good writers.

At the Joseph Warren Beach residence, party-goers also found a different Lewis.[27] There were no verbal exchanges, no fencing. Instead, a sick old man, shaking badly, placed an ashtray on his lap and used both hands to hold it still. He was extremely quiet, no longer stormy or opinionated. All the guests were quick to recognize his decline, and not one challenged him to an argument. Instead, they pitied him.

For Lewis, it was time to move on again. He had grown tired of the city and the city had grown tired of him. As he recorded in his diary:

> How a Sauk Centre can be the center of the universe. Brenda Ueland's story of the man from Podunk, New York or Pekin, symphonies or Corning glass, a university class in Sanskrit or a German-English war—what have they for a man in Sauk Centre, he unconsciously asks himself. And there is everything there: friends, enemies, work, love, home, bed, cigars, ham, fishing and fishing tackle, shoes, pencils, music— once in Eastern Star recital and now on radio, church and hence God, and a railroad station at which he could take train for steamers to Rome—if he wanted to.[28]

SINCLAIR LEWIS SITES IN MINNEAPOLIS

54. Sinclair Lewis residence: 1801 James Avenue South.
55. Sinclair Lewis residence: 1500 Mount Curve Avenue.
56. Arthur Upson residence: 1217 First Avenue South (razed).
57. Arthur Upson residence: 916 Fifth Avenue South (razed).
58. Arthur Upson residence: 69 South Eleventh Street, flat 15 (razed).
59. Arthur Upson residence: 1779 James Avenue South.
60. Joseph Warren Beach residence: 1801 University Avenue SE.
61. Carlton Miles residence: 2412 Aldrich Avenue South.
62. Karl Andrist residence: 706 Delaware SE (razed).
63. Hotel Maryland (Sinclair Lewis): 1346 LaSalle Avenue South.
64. Leamington Hotel (William McNally): Tenth Street and Third Avenue South.
65. John Cowles residence: 2318 Park Avenue South.
66. F. Peavey Heffelfinger residence: Wayzata (razed).
67. Addison Lewis residence: Long Lake.
68. Alfred Wilson residence: 4704 Townes Road, Edina.
69. Minneapolis Institute of Arts: Twenty-fourth Street and Stevens Avenue South.

70. Virginia Lewis residence: 1802 Colfax Avenue South.
71. Dorothy Bennett residence: 2024 Penn Avenue South.
72. Frederick Wheeler house: 1800 Dupont Avenue South.
73. Sinclair Lewis college classroom: 301 Folwell Hall, University of Minnesota.
74. Robert Penn Warren residence: 3124 West Calhoun Boulevard, apartment 405.
75. Ione Jackson residence: 158 Bedford Street.
76. John Baxter residence: 1779 Girard Avenue South.
77. Frederick Manfred residence: 1076 Eighteenth Avenue SE.
78. Frederick Manfred residence: 1814 SE Fourth Street (razed).
79. Frederick Manfred residence: 6717 Auto Club Road.
80. James Roers residence: 3141 Sixteenth Avenue South.
81. Meridel LeSueur residence: 2521 Harriet Avenue South (razed).
82. Brenda Ueland residence: 3820 West Calhoun Boulevard.
83. Sigurd Ueland residence: 3832 Richfield Avenue.
84. Rolf Ueland residence: 3846 Richfield Avenue.
85. Arnulf Ueland residence: 3850 Richfield Avenue.
86. Dr. Anna Augusta Von Helmholtz Phelan residence: 5315 Woodlawn Boulevard.
87. Barbara Bell residence: 1205 Lincoln Avenue.
88. Donald Simmons residence: Wayzata.

Virginia Lewis home, 1802 Colfax Avenue South, Minneapolis. Sinclair's niece Virginia lived in this house in 1942 and the author's timely advice helped shape her future. Photograph by Constance Gunnufson, 1980.

89. Helen Baxter residence: 4601 Fremont Avenue South.
90. Kate Wood residence: 2011 Third Avenue South.
91. Rufus Rand, Jr., residence: 4551 East Lake Harriet Boulevard.
92. John Dalrymple residence: 2327 Pillsbury Avenue South.
93. Lewis Daniel residence: 4111 Linden Hills Boulevard.
94. David Shearer residence: 1929 Kenwood Parkway.
95. Alan Shearer residence: 2502 West Twenty-second Street.
96. Rufus Rand, Jr., residence: 1800 Dupont Avenue South.
97. Alan Shearer residence: 1912 Queen Avenue South.
98. Harold Sweatt residence: Crystal Bay.

6

Mankato

I am here in this Minnesota town for the summer—and I like it, like the friendliness, the neighborliness, and the glorious sweeps of country round about.[1]

ON JUNE 1, 1919, Lewis, Grace, and Wells moved into the J. W. Schmitt house on South Broad Street in Mankato, Minnesota.[2]. The Schmitts had been abroad, and upon their return they occupied their fashionable summer house on nearby Lake Washington, leaving their Broad Street residence to the Lewises.

Sinclair Lewis house, 315 So. Broad Street, Mankato, Minnesota. Lewis rented the J. W. Schmitt house on June 1, 1919 and worked on both Free Air and Main Street here. Photograph by Joseph Wise, 1979.

69

Lewis was impressed by the well-constructed brick house furnished with late Grant and early Garfield furniture, the beautiful elm-shaded streets, the curious shops, and, above all, the friendly people. In Minneapolis, residents had been perpetually on guard, but here in the sanctuary of Mankato, Lewis and his family were regarded simply as "folks," and they relished the tranquility of small-town Minnesota.

The Schmitts extended Lewis a two-month lease on the house but charged him no rent; Schmitt permitted him to occupy the house simply because he liked him.[3] The home was a godsend to Lewis, who had been searching for a place to write, and the pleasant Minnesota summer permitted Wells to have a sleeping crib set up on the porch.

Marcia T. Schuster, director of the Blue Earth County Historical Society, describes Mankato as it was that summer of 1919:

> The Great War was over. But amid the rejoicing, returning veterans were having trouble finding jobs. . . . Mankato citizens could not agree on an appropriate permanent memorial; one suggestion was to plant Victory elms. . . . The newspapers printed many letters from "our boys" overseas. . . . A victory pageant was scheduled for July 4. . . . The Army was recruiting for occupation forces in Germany. . . . The Red Cross was collecting used clothing. . . . Prohibition was enforced. . . . Liberty Load subscriptions totalled $394,700. . . . Mankato's population was 15,000, while the Census Bureau also announced that one marriage in nine ended in divorce. . . . A local man was arrested for making seditious remarks.[4]

Lewis may or may not have been aware that a man had been arrested for making seditious remarks in Mankato, but after his own unpleasant experiences in both St. Paul and Minneapolis, where his own actions and remarks had ruined him, he was determined to be less opinionated in this sleeping little town on the Minnesota River. Mrs. Schuster continues:

> Horses and buggies shared the muddy roads with the automobile. . . . Special patrols were set up to catch the speedsters clocked at 35 miles per hour. . . . Driver's License examiners were to come to Mankato to give tests instead of the motorist having to travel to St. Paul to be examined. . . . The road departments were making plans to hard-surface the roads and there was talk that auto stealing should be made a crime just as horse stealing was. . . . The city announced plans to install sidewalks.

Lewis had selected this small town as an ideal location to revamp *Free Air*, which had been serialized in the *Saturday Evening Post* from May 31 through June 21. He considered Mankato ideal because it was far removed from the clamor and bustle of the city and not as clannish as his native Sauk Centre, where everyone in the town recognized him. In Mankato, he was acquainted with practically no one, so there was little danger of old friends dropping by to interrupt his writing. Because it was larger than Sauk Centre, Mankato appeared free of the normal small-town gossip that was so painfully evident in his hometown.

To isolate himself from his wife and baby so he could write, he rented office space in the Fred W. Kruse Building, choosing the back room of a photographer's studio, which overlooked the railroad yards.[5] In addition to reshaping *Free Air*, Lewis worked on his serious offering, *Main Street*, which he had struggled with in Minneapolis. The townsfolk, aware of the type of book he was writing, wondered if they'd be used as characters in the novel.

Lewis's books, like his actions, had the effect of getting him into trouble. This time, the Mankato newspapers came to his rescue.[6] His heroine in *Free Air*, while negotiating a stretch of highway running west out of the Twin Cities, buried her car in mud and had to be pulled out several times. The *St. Paul Dispatch*, irked by his degrading of Minnesota roads, rose to the defense of the highways.[7] The *Dispatch* attributed the "inaccuracy" to "journalistic license." But many readers, especially those who were frequent travelers, sided with Lewis. In a letter to the editor of the *Dispatch* (which later was reprinted in the *Mankato Daily Free Press*), one reader stated:

> I am tempted to invite the certain member of your editorial staff who wrote caustic criticism of Sinclair Lewis's "Free Air" story in the Saturday Evening Post to accompany me on a tour of enlightenment over the "arterial road" of this state toward the Dakota line. Last week I drove to Mankato and saw three machines stuck between Bell[e] Plaine and LeSueur. The road to Lake Crystal was fair, but when we plunged out into the quaking quagmire, which is dignified by being called the Main Road, we put her in the second and actually plowed along for two miles dragging the apron.
>
> Of course we are fixing them up, but that does not alter the fact that Sinclair Lewis's description in the Saturday Evening Post was and is accurate, and that such roads as described are existent in this state and in no sense a flight of the author's imagination.[8]

Over half a column of space in the *Dispatch* was devoted to readers who defended Lewis's remarks and who agreed that Minnesota's roads were in dire need of repair. That many of these roads were nearly impassable was evidenced by an article that appeared in the *Mankato Daily Free Press* on June 2, 1919:

> Motorists who drove on the Lake Madison road yesterday complained of a bad mud hole in the road, after the turn north from the corner east of Eagle Lake. Several automobiles came to grief at this place yesterday.

A nervous reporter from the Mankato paper went to interview Lewis, bringing with him a copy of the St. Paul paper. Lewis perused the article and granted the cub an interview; the young reporter was astonished to find him such a willing subject. "Journalistic license indeed," muttered the author, who had driven that same road himself and had also been mired in the mud. While the reporter waited, Lewis dashed off a sharp reply.

The *Mankato Daily Review* displayed the following banner headline the next day: "Sinclair Lewis is a Booster for Good Roads. Author of Story in SEP Calls Attention to Minnesota Roads."[9] He was quoted as saying: "I believe that just because we are campaigning for the better roads amendment, it helps rather than hinders to call attention to the fact that our roads are not perfect."

This statement was composed by Lewis in Mankato, in the form of a reply to a letter from Harry G. Davis, secretary of the Minnesota Highway Improvement Association, who disagreed with the analysis of Minnesota roads in *Free Air*. Lewis went on to say:

> First of all please understand that I am a Minnesotan by birth and present residence, and that I want tourists to come here, quite as much for their own sake as for Minnesota's sake. And it is my hope and belief that Free Air is much more likely to bring them here than to turn them away. . . .
>
> The road from Minneapolis here to Mankato (I drove it one week ago) is almost impassable after rains, whether you go by way of Shakopee—which the T.I.B. gives as a main highway—or by way of Faribault. Between Faribault and here a friend of mine recently was stuck three times and had to be hauled out.

Lewis concluded by praising the country road from Sauk Centre to Wadena and hypothesized that if all roads in the state were up to par, tourists would come to appreciate our hills, prairies, lakes, and woods and would not have to be disturbed by such hazards as bad roads.

Besides a crusade for better roads in Minnesota, Lewis also supported the popular Chautauqua movement (similar to the Lyceum
movement), which had been established in 1874. Offering courses in
art, science, and the humanities, its authors, explorers, musicians, and
political leaders were dispatched to lecture, and a variety of entertain-
ment was furnished as well.

During the summer Lewis spent in Mankato, the town was visited
by the famous Italian band, the Banda Roma; a flight instructor doing
exhibitions; a cast presenting the play *The Melting Pot*; a jazz band
known as Dunbar's White Hussars; the Boston Opera Singers;
humorist Ralph "Bing" Bingham; Kryl's Saxophone Sextette; famed
lecturer Charles S. Medbury; Maj. Ray C. Bridgman, holder of the
American record for actual flight hours above German lines; Red
Cross nurse Mary K. Nelson; Gov. George A. Carlson, "The Fighting
Swede"; "Creed of American Bolshevism" authority Frank Dixon;
Chicago detective Harry J. Loose; the Althea Players (violinists);
young actors performing *The Pied Piper of Hamelin*; poet Wallace
Bruce Amsbary; and a Mesopotamian descendant of kings, Raphael
Emmanuel.[10]

Like many others, Lewis went to see Sir John Foster Fraser, Great
Britain's foremost journalist, who had just traveled from the Paris
Peace Conference to deliver a powerful address in Mankato June
24–30 for the Chautauqua Institute. According to one Mankato newspaper, "No man in the world is better qualified to discuss the great
problems of world politics than is Sir John. . . . [He] comes to
Chautauqua from the Paris Peace Conference with a great address on
remaking the map of the world." Additional billing stated that "he has
traveled in more than fifty countries and enjoyed the personal ac-
quaintanceship of most of the statesmen and diplomats of the
world."[11]

Culture was not new to the citizens of Mankato, as Mankato resident Anna Wiecking related in an undated letter to scholar H. O.
Lokensgard:

> Citizens of Mankato have long interested themselves in cul-
> tural matters. As early as 1853 a Lyceum course brought to
> village audiences "learned addresses, fiery debates, and in-
> spiring songs." During the 1870s, some of the famous people
> who entertained in Mankato's lecture halls were Wendell
> Phillips, Bayard Taylor, Henry Ward Beecher, Edward
> Eggelston, Karl Schurz and the Mendelssohn Club of Boston.
> In the Opera House, built in 1882 (it stood where near the
> American Legion Building stands today), appeared such

celebrities as Madame Modjeska, Robert Mantell, Chauncey Alcott, to name a few.

From beneath the overheated tent of the Chautauqua, Lewis frequently rescued some of the perspiring lecturers, leading them to his house on Broad Street for a much-needed drink.[12]

As Lewis serviced the thirsty staff of the Chautauqua, Grace took a shine to Stella Louise Wood, a teacher Grace met in Minneapolis earlier that same year.[13] Grace had attended Miss Wood's course in psychology and had accompanied her on visits to several schools.

Miss Wood came to Mankato to celebrate Wells' second birthday and suggested that the Lewises construct three small steps against a tree trunk and add a seesaw plank on which the child could play.[14] With the completion of the new playground, other inquisitive children in the neighborhood came to play, and Wells acquired his first playmates. Lewis frequently delayed the jaunt to his office to observe his contented son.

Numerous were the picnics and swimming parties at Madison Lake, a prestigious resort community ten miles northeast of Mankato. The Point Pleasant Hotel, the most popular resort on the lake, boasted many famous guests, and Mankato's most prosperous families—the Pattersons, the Meaghers, the Owens, the Hubbards, the Wises, and the Rays—had cottages there.

An advertisement in the *Mankato Daily Review* on July 17, 1919, stated: "Good swimming beach, illuminated by searchlight, 20 tickets $1.00. Boats and canoes by the hour. Point Pleasant Hotel Pavilion, Madison Lake, Minnesota."

But it was to the Schmitt cottage on Lake Washington that the Lewises came every Sunday night, rain or shine, invited or uninvited.[15] When the Lewises arrived, the Schmitt children were always asked to occupy themselves on the front lawn, which abutted a high, steep slope down to the lake. Lewis always insisted on assisting with the cooking of dinner and the subsequent wiping of dishes. The maids were always off on Sundays, so the Lewises and the Schmitts worked together at the chores. After the Lewises left, Mr. Schmitt often complained of the rapid depletion of his wines and corn whiskeys.

The Schmitt children loved "Uncle Sin" and considered him the most delightful grownup they knew. He had a knack for relating to children and would lie on his back in the grass with the children beside him and look for shooting stars, reach for fireflies, and create humorous, ridiculous songs that he taught them to sing.

At a party both the Lewises and Schmitts attended, a young Schmitt daughter was requested to provide piano accompaniment for Mankato composer Clara Gerlach Edwards, who had written a popular song, "By the Bend in the River." Miss Edwards could not play the piano, and she would hum her melodies to a ghost composer in New York City, who would then add the lyrics. Lewis behaved himself as the Schmitt girl played flawlessly in a pretty gown but barefooted.

Lewis was extremely fond of cookies. He in fact concocted his own recipe, which he gave to Mrs. Schmitt. From that time on, he always expected his favorite cookies when he arrived. The recipe for "Sin Lewis's Sinful Christmas Cookies" was as follows:

½ pound butter
½ cup almonds, finely chopped
2 cups sugar
2 tablespoons Drostes Cocoa
2 eggs
1 shot glass bourbon
2 cups bread flour
Roll out very thin on floured board and cut with cookie cutters. Bake on well-greased tins at 375 degrees.

With or without his cookies, Lewis quickly struck up acquaintances with other Mankato residents, including Mr. and Mrs. Charles Butler, who owned the *Free Press*; Fred Kruse, who operated a clothing business; and Leo Carney, who was in the cement business.[16] They were all members of the Elks Club, and Lewis played cards there regularly and crashed their closed parties.

He longed to be a part of that group but was regarded by some as an ugly, acne-faced, eccentric writer; he remained always on the periphery. He sometimes was invited to club events, but when he wasn't, he often appeared uninvited to the disdain of club officials. Many felt he had taken advantage of the Schmitt's generosity, for, when they returned from abroad, they found all their wine bottles filled with water.

Lewis continually masterminded things to get attention. When an acquaintance of his, Frank P. Hoerr, entertained guests at a garden party and invited the Lewises, Harry, never one to be punctual, arrived late on a tandem bicycle with Grace.

At a party hosted by Mrs. Leo Carney, guests were seated in the living room when, suddenly, they looked up to find Lewis descending the staircase, wearing one of Mrs. Carney's formal gowns. He casually chatted with guests as if nothing extraordinary had occurred. Mrs.

Carney, shocked that he had entered her bedroom and put on her clothing, never wore the gown again.

On another occasion, Mr. and Mrs. Braden Clemens were comfortably seated on their front porch, when they noticed a figure crawling on the sidewalk. Slowly the man ascended the stairs and crouched before Mrs. Clemens. With a look of anguish on his face, Lewis begged, "Oh, lady, do you have a drink for a thirsty man?"

Lewis saw much of Frank Crandall and William Browder, two bachelors who lived next door.[17] Both men relished tomfoolery, and Lewis was only too willing to partake in the merrymaking. He also enjoyed chats with Father Hughes of St. John's Irish Catholic Church, with whom he relished debating atheism.

Lewis was introduced to Mr. and Mrs. Lee Wood at a reception given by a Mrs. Andrews.[18] The Woods tolerated his caustic behavior and found his habit of crashing parties amusing. The Lewises frequently would drop in on the Woods unexpectedly, and they all would depart for swimming sessions at the Schmitt cottage on Lake Washington.

Another friend, Thomas Edwards, a Mankato salesman, frequently met Lewis at the Schmitt parties and for fishing expeditions at Lake Washington.[19] During their initial encounter, Edwards failed to recognize him because, in contrast to the Lewis that Edwards had heard about, he seemed decent, natural, and unpretentious. The Lewises grew fond of his Norwegian stories and begged him to repeat them time and time again.

Edwards and others in Mankato wondered why Lewis frequently sported a monocle. The monocle was an oddity, worn because Lewis craved attention and was a chronic practical joker. Everyone there knew he had been in London, and they felt that anyone who would crawl on sidewalks, wear a woman's gown, and ride a tandem bicycle could sport a monocle if he so desired.

There was also a serious side to this monocled invader. Lewis's erratic behavior was often questionable, but he did have a genuine concern for his community. With social services and welfare nonexistent, Lewis brought a donation of children's clothing to the back door of Mrs. H. R. Wiecking's home for the Women's Relief Society.[20] The volunteer group gave food and clothing to the needy at Christmas. Mrs. Wiecking was touched to find a set of Wells' white booties included with the Lewis donation.

Lewis spent considerable time at the MacBeth Livery Stable, talking with its proprietor, John MacBeth. Another frequent visitor was Father Hughes.[21] These unlikely companions, seating themselves on the sidewalk in front of the livery, tilted their chairs against the wall and conversed for hours on topics ranging from politics to religion.

MacBeth often would hitch a bobtail pacer to an attractive runabout, and Lewis would disappear for hours in the countryside. He liked to explore the country surrounding Mankato, for he had roots in this region and so did Carol Kennicott. This was Carol's country, and he longed to see what Carol saw, what his own grandparents had seen, and it was only fitting that he might see by horse rather than by car what the others once had glimpsed.

Lewis was writing *Free Air* and *Main Street*, but he possibly had commenced planning *Arrowsmith* in Mankato.[22] He was deeply interested in the Southern Minnesota Medical Association, of which Mr. Schmitt was a member. The group's meetings in Mankato and Rochester, at which famous medical practitioners spoke, interested him deeply.

Lewis discussed his own medical background with Schmitt—his physician father and brother and many other relatives and friends. Lewis informed him of his interest in both the Southern Minnesota Medical Association and the Mayo Clinic and pleaded with Schmitt to allow him to accompany him to Rochester to attend one of the association's meetings. Schmitt consented and took both Harry and Grace to Rochester.

In Rochester, Lewis mesmerized the Schmitt children with his keen sense of perception. Walking down the main street of the city en route to the medical banquet, Lewis pointed to a portly, short, middle-aged man directly in front of them. Lewis nudged young Margaret Schmitt. "Margaret, do you know what kind of cane that man is carrying?" he asked. Margaret responded negatively. "Well, it is a whiskey cane," he replied. "Let's sit next to it and see what happens."

At the banquet, the Lewises and the Schmitts positioned themselves at the same table as Dr. Beebe of St. Cloud, the gentleman with the cane. Lewis introduced himself to Dr. Beebe, and since his brother was also a physician in St. Cloud, he was quickly able to strike up a conversation. After dessert, Lewis leaned forward and asked Beebe if his cane contained the requisite "*spiritis fermenta*." This it did, and Beebe unscrewed the top and withdrew a liquor glass, which he filled and passed around the table.

If Lewis shocked more than a few members of the medical association, he also shocked Mankato residents with his outspoken demeanor. In an *Atlantic Monthly* article by Perry Miller, Lewis was quoted as saying, "I love America but I don't like her." This statement enraged many Americans, especially those who had recently served in the war or had lost a relative in it. Lewis explained he did not intend that the statement be taken in a narrow, mean sense but in Kipling's sense of "for there is neither East nor West, nor border, nor breed, nor birth, when two strong men stand face to face though they come from the ends of the earth."

Outspoken he may have been, but people wanted to hear him speak. That summer he lectured at the local college and discussed the uses and abuses of the short story. On July 30, 1919, the *Mankato Daily Free Press* ran the following article covering Lewis's speaking engagement:

> In speaking of the authors and literary offerings in the United States, Mr. Lewis had few, if any words of praise, but stated that the time is rapidly passing when the nation can satisfy itself with being a mediocre nation in literature.
>
> He spoke of fiction as "contemporary history", and explained how, when true to life, it reveals people as they are. In speaking of the SEP, for which he has written fiction, he explained that it was the policy of the Post to publish stories about real people and characters that are familiar to everyone, the writers taking ordinary people and investing them with the glamour of fiction, until even a bootblack will appear interesting and be recognized as a real person with aspirations, hopes and fears.

He went on to criticize popular American authors like Rex Beach, whose characters he considered unreal, and he demonstrated by contrast how realistic everyday characters could be when portrayed by an author who wrote about life as it really was. In all his novels and short stories, he had written about real people in real situations, but because of this realism he had managed to offend many.

The *Mankato Daily Review* also quoted Lewis's speech in their July 30, 1919, issue:

> "I said that in this country the novelists and writers shy clear of writing about the things of real importance in social structure and do not take things seriously enough."
>
> In spite of the warm weather Mr. Lewis was greeted by a good sized audience last night, made up of not only summer school students but a number of town people who took advantage of the opportunity to listen to a really brilliant man and worthwhile writer and of whom Mankato may feel proud of having had in their midst.

The article contained Lewis's boast that the novel would soon cease to be looked upon merely as fiction, but would become the medium that would introduce readers to the significant problems confronting society. He ventured that preacher Billy Sunday would soon topple in popularity and that writers like Rex Beach and Harold Bell Wright would soon fall from popularity, making room for realists like Edith Wharton, Frank Norris, H. G. Wells, Joseph Conrad, Joseph Hergesheimer, Theodore Dreiser, Harold Fredericks, and Compton MacKenzie. He elaborated on the difficulties encountered by authors determined to become master craftsmen, and he stated that writers were made, not born—that they were products of years of hard work.

During this lecture at Mankato Teachers College, it was evident to some that Lewis was weary: He talked much too fast and acted as if he didn't wish to speak at all.[23] Grace, seated in the audience, appeared alarmed over his quick delivery and whispered to him, "Slower, slower."

The summer passed quickly. According to Marcia T. Schuster:

> The first woman to fly over Mankato appeared July 4. . . . A man estimated his wife's worth at $50,000. . . . The women celebrated the anniversary of granting suffrage to Wyoming women in 1869. . . . There were cases of influenza and a scourge of grasshoppers. . . . The ice harvest was held up and a famine predicted until Mankato was able to secure ice from Rochester. . . . There were reports of coasting down Walnut Street hill. . . . Plans were announced to build a clubhouse at the Mankato Golf Club for $10,000 to be ready July 1. . . . A combined Ringling Brothers and Barnum and Bailey Circus would come to Mankato soon.

As aviators, circuses, and new golf clubs came to Mankato, so did Lewis's parents. The newspaper quickly ran a notice in the personal section: "Dr. and Mrs. Lewis of Sauk Centre, Minnesota, are visiting in the city as the guests of their son Sinclair Lewis and family on South Broad Street."[24]

Two days later, the *Mankato Daily Review*, in its "Social Circles" section, chronicled a dinner party for twenty-four guests at the Point Pleasant Hotel in Madison Lake in honor of Dr. and Mrs. Edwin Lewis.[25] The Point Pleasant was the finest hostelry in the area. Lewis gave his parents a grand tour of Mankato and also took them to nearby Elysian to visit relatives.[26]

After his parents returned to Sauk Centre, Lewis suddenly became discontented.[27] As work on *Main Street* grew more intense, he began to feel more lonely; he longed for friends who would sit and wrangle over two-hour lunches or walk with him in the late afternoon after writing sessions. Mankato Rotarians were simply too busy. He had grown weary of hearing about motor cars and crops. He and Grace decided they had to escape.

Lewis reassured himself that he had accomplished what he had set out to do. He had revamped *Free Air* and set the world straight on Minnesota roads, and he had given some substance to *Main Street*, even though that progress had ground to an abrupt halt.

The *Mankato Daily Review* recorded his departure from the city:

> Sinclair Lewis and family, who have been spending the summer at the J. W. Schmitt home in this city, will leave Thursday for the East where they will spend the winter. They will make their trip by auto and plan to go by way of Kentucky, Virginia and Pennsylvania.[28]

Citizens at Elks Club meetings and Sunday brunches dissected his rapid departure and the impact he had had on them.[29] Lewis kept ties with the few Mankato cronies he had. He told Ferdinand Hoerr (Frank's brother) in a letter dated August 28, 1920, and mailed from Kennebago Lake, Maine, that he often thought of Mankato, the people, the parties, and the sunsets from the bluff at Jack Schmitt's. He continued:

> The last ten months I've been working night and day on a novel, to be called "Main Street", and to be published by Harcourt, Brace and Howe of NY about October 10th. It will not be serialized in any magazine. It's much the best thing I've ever done. The scene of most of the story is in a small prairie town somewhere toward the northern part of Minnesota (it's no town in particular but a composite of a number of them). But I have the heroine born in Mankato, and there are two descriptions of the loveliness and general agreeableness of Mankato, as contrasted with the flat prairie towns.

In another letter to Hoerr, dated February 24, 1921, Lewis informed him that a friend of his, Ruby Cravens, who had appeared in *Hobohemia*, was coming to Mankato with the Nightie-Night Company March 13. He implored Hoerr to throw a party honoring her.

> They will be in Winona March 9th; Faribault, the 10th; Owatonna, the 11th; Rochester, the 12th; and Mankato, the 13th. I hope the town is getting some very good advertising out of its

mention in "Main Street" which has now sold way over one hundred thousand.

Mankato residents would not soon forget him or, in many cases, forgive him, but some of his friends, including Charles Butler, received autographed copies of *Free Air* in the mail shortly after his departure. The inscription read:

> I wish I could send all of Mankato my new book—because I like Mankato just a little better than any other town in the world—and because I wrote the last half of this book there. But since I can't [word omitted] a copy to everybody, I send this to all of Mankato in care of Charley Butler and the *Free Press*. But I'll let you all off easily. I shan't expect the *Free Press* to devote more than nine pages to boosting it. I shan't expect Fred Kruse and Lee Carney and all the rest to buy more than four copies each. But I shall expect the Elk's Club at lunch to say, "I hear Lewis has written a book. Huh? No sir! Don't lend me a copy! I'm going to buy one." (Comment from Charley: "What you expect and what you'll get are something else again"). But anyway—here's to Mankato—all of it! [30]

Nearly three decades later, in 1947, Sinclair Lewis was temporarily living in St. Paul, researching his historical novel, *The God-Seeker*. He traveled to Mankato to uncover new information. A nervous desk clerk at the Ben Pay Hotel in Mankato called the newsroom of the *Free Press* and informed an editor that Sinclair Lewis had just checked in. [31] A frightened young reporter, Ken Berg, sought an interview with the noted author and knocked on Lewis's door.
"Who the hell is it?"
Berg identified himself.
"Go the hell away."
The dejected reporter sat for two hours in the hotel lobby, hoping to tackle the author when he came down, but Lewis never appeared. Berg gave up and returned to his office.
A younger Lewis would have welcomed the attention and gone out of his way to say something shocking, but he craved no publicity in 1947. There was no longer any need to shock people; he was merely passing through Mankato, St. Paul, Minneapolis, and Sauk Centre, researching a book he knew would never be a hit and taking a final look at places he had once, however briefly, called home. The steamer to Rome would soon depart; Lewis gave Minnesota a last, tearful glance and remembered that this was the stuff of *Main Street*.

SINCLAIR LEWIS SITES IN MANKATO

99. Sinclair Lewis residence: 315 South Broad Street.
100. Sinclair Lewis office: F. W. Kruse Building, 417–19 South Front Street.
101. John MacBeth house: 315 South Hickory.
102. MacBeth Livery Stable: 205 Hickory (razed).
103. H. R. Wiecking residence: 506 Byron Street.
104. Charles Butler and Braden Clemens residence: 704 South Broad Street.
105. Fred W. Kruse residence: 130 Parsons Street.
106. Leo Carney residence: 612 Baker Street.
107. Frank P. Hoerr residence: 1603 North Broad Street.
108. Elks Club: 129 East Hickory (razed).
109. Schmitt summer home: Lake Washington off Route 2 (razed).
110. Point Pleasant Hotel: Madison Lake (razed).

7

Elysian-Waterville

Cemetery at Elysian, Minnesota, near Mankato. Coming out of prairie country, but rolling, this graveyard is on a wooded bluff overlooking Lake Elysian. It is truly rural. Fresh lilacs, plucked, on a grave, give a sweet odor. Many cedars.[1]

FARMER JOHN LEWIS married Emeline Johnson in Connecticut in 1836, and the family moved to Elysian, Minnesota, in 1866.[2] They quickly erected a homestead on Cleveland Road, between Lake Francis and Schoolhouse Lake. Three children were born to the John Lewises: Martha A. (1843–83), Edwin J. (1848–1926), and Emma A. (dates unknown).

The oldest, Martha A. Lewis, married Frank M. Long, a Civil War veteran, in 1871, and they lived on a farm in Greenland, Minnesota, two miles west of Elysian. Long had volunteered soon after the outbreak of the Civil War in 1861; when he later journeyed to Minnesota and established a community, he used the name of his hometown, Greenland, Ohio.[3] Long purchased a two-hundred-acre farm and operated his own sawmill on the property.[4] Four children were born. Martha died in 1883, when her youngest child was three years old. Long later remarried.

Sinclair Lewis's father, Edwin J., was a schoolteacher in Elysian. In 1873 he married Emma F. Kermott, a schoolteacher from Waseca. Shortly after their marriage, he left Elysian to teach school in Redwood Falls, where he became interested in medicine. When Edwin Lewis went away to study medicine at Rush Medical College in Chicago, Emma and their son, Fred, lodged with John and Emeline Lewis in Elysian.

The youngest child born to the John Lewises at Elysian was Emma. She later married Loren Williams, also of Elysian, and two children were born: Forrest Lewis Williams and Guy Williams.

Thus, many of Sinclair Lewis's relatives resided in Elysian: Frank

The graves of John and Emeline Lewis in Cedar Hill Cemetery, Elysian, Minnesota. The grandparents of Sinclair Lewis, moved to Elysian in 1866. Sinclair made pilgrimages to their graves in both 1919 and 1942. Photographed by Joseph Wise, 1979.

Long's sister, Carrie, operated a small country store in Greenland and lived next door.[5] Most of these relatives in the Elysian-Greenland area took offense some years later to Lewis's novel *Elmer Gantry*—especially Frank Long's second wife, who was a devoted Methodist.

During the summer of 1919, Sinclair Lewis was living in nearby Mankato. Just before he left the city, his parents visited, and the family embarked on a short motor trip to Elysian to visit Sinclair's cousin Forrest Williams and his wife, Edith.[6] Edwin's brother-in-law, Loren, was also at the house, and Harry created quite a stir in town by arriving in a classy touring car and garbed in a duster.[7]

Everyone in the community was proud to have a celebrity in his midst, especially after the controversy caused by Lewis's attack on Minnesota roads in *Free Air*. In addition to visiting the Williamses, Harry, Grace, Wells, Edwin, and Isabel paid a visit to the Long cousins in Greenland.[8] In 1919 Greenland consisted of a church, a grain elevator, and a general store, which was run as a cooperative.[9] The town always had been very small and was continually threatened with extinction. Many of the farmers in the Greenland-Elysian area regularly attended meetings of the Nonpartisan League, a group of great interest to Lewis, who found the movement an important one. He

Sinclair Lewis at St. Michael Cemetery in St. Michael, Minnesota around 1942. Lewis often borrowed the names of characters for his fiction from actual tombstones. Photograph courtesy Isabel Lewis Agrell and Virginia Lewis.

attended meetings of the league in Mankato and Elysian and also frequented some league picnics.

After his visits to the Williamses and Longs, Lewis made a pilgrimage to the family burial plot in Cedar Hill Cemetery.[10] He came seeking information about his paternal grandparents. As was his habit, he also scrutinized other monuments in the graveyard, constantly searching the tombstones for names that could be used for characters in his novels.

Lewis was so haunted by the gray tombstones at Cedar Hill he was reluctant to leave the cemetery. He dreamed about these neglected tombstones throughout his life and vowed to return someday when he had more time to ponder the stories the stones told.

On May 10, 1942, Lewis, then a Minnesota resident with a spacious summer home in Excelsior, kept his promise and returned to Cedar Hill Cemetery after a twenty-three-year hiatus.[11] He discovered that he still was spooked by the curious headstones and noted that most of the stones were of polished red or gray granite, which had come into vogue since his grandfather's marble and the then-modern soft, rough granite with chased lettering.

He was astonished to discover an absence of religious inscriptions on the headstones, and came to the conclusion that the town was probably not very religious, although relatives in this same community had once taken offense to his knocking of religion in *Elmer Gantry*.

He was deeply touched by the grave of a nineteen-year-old bride named Sarah Fish, who had died three years before the Minnesota Sioux Uprising of 1862. He stooped over the headstone and deciphered the following message, inscribed in granite:

> Rest thee, loved one, where we laid thee,
> Where the wild wood maketh sigh,
> Tears perfume the bed we made thee,
> Where the withered foliage lie.

He could only guess what had befallen her husband, Hiram, and he searched for his headstone in the maze of cold granite. Unable to locate a marker bearing the name of Hiram Fish, he wondered if the husband had journeyed West or had remarried. He pondered what both Hiram and Sarah Fish might have looked like and even counted the days young Sarah had lived. He thought of his friends in New York and how they would regard him as a sentimental old fool if they could have seen him. He could not refrain from digging into the past but persisted in his efforts to discover his own roots and the roots of other Minnesotans. These were the people he wished to write about.

Lewis wrote about Minnesota landscapes throughout his life; his friend Adolph Dehn painted them. Dehn had been born November 22, 1895, in Waterville, Minnesota, just down the road from Elysian.[12] Like Lewis, Dehn was a reformer and both were interested in such progressive movements as the Nonpartisan League.

The two had met in New York through a humorous telephone conversation. Dehn had never met Lewis, but one day his telephone rang and a voice boomed: "This is Sinclair Lewis speaking. As a fellow Minnesotan I'd like very much to come over and see your Minnesota paintings."[13]

Dehn cautiously replied: "Come over by all means. But, pardon me, my friends are always pulling my leg and I'm not sure you're Sinclair Lewis. Whoever you are, I'll be glad to see you."

Lewis was at a loss to prove his identity. Verbal sparring ensued. The two compared notes on mutual friends until Dehn was finally convinced that his caller was indeed Sinclair Lewis. Lewis came over, and the two reminisced about Minnesota. They even planned to collaborate on some books.

Lewis and Dehn hoped to drive a van across the country in search of the real America.[14] Together they would seek the Watervilles, the

Adolph Dehn birthplace, 221 North Herbert Street, Waterville, Minnesota. A famous painter and friend of Sinclair Lewis, Dehn was born in this house November 22, 1895. Photograph by Joseph Wise, 1979.

Elysians, and the Sauk Centres that composed the nation's backbone. They would record their experiences in a book. Lewis would write, and Dehn would paint his American landscapes. Alas, their plans never materialized, but neither man ever relinquished his dream of discovering the real America.

Lewis did purchase some of Dehn's paintings.[15] "He looked at all my Minnesota scenes but wasn't interested in landscapes outside the state, or pictures of anything non-Minnesota," Dehn later said.[16]

Dehn's experience illustrates Lewis's genuine devotion to the state of his birth. Even more telling were Lewis's visits to Cedar Hill Cemetery. Sensing a kinship with the tombstones, he was like the narrator in Alexander Pope's classic poem, "Solitude," who sought something more significant than a mere physical homecoming:

> Happy the man, whose wish and care
> A few paternal acres bound,
> Content to breathe his native air
>   In his own ground.

SINCLAIR LEWIS SITES IN ELYSIAN

111. John Lewis residence: Cleveland Road on Lake Francis (razed).
112. Frank Long residence: Old Highway 60.
113. Forrest Williams residence: Beaver Dam Road (now County Road 11), razed.
114. Cedar Hill Cemetery: Just off Highway 60.

SINCLAIR LEWIS SITE IN WATERVILLE

115. Adolph Dehn birthplace: 221 North Herbert Street.

8

Saskatchewan

Suddenly they were in the calm waters beyond the rapids, and in relief Ralph sobbed above his lifted paddle, so that the girl looked back in wonder, and the Indian snickered. There was a sacred moment of security. But always Ralph knew that they were fleeing from the angry man who might be following them—angry and swift and menacing.[1]

DURING THE WINTER of 1923–24, Sinclair Lewis secured permission to accompany one of the Indian treaty party trips dispatched yearly by the Canadian government.[2] There were twelve such expeditions, which covered the Indian territory in northern Canada from Labrador to the Mackenzie River.[3] Duncan G. Scott, director of Indian affairs in Ottawa, selected trip number ten for Lewis and his party.

Lewis had heard much about the expeditions. Since he considered his own life lacking in adventure, he decided to participate in such a trip to chronicle the events on paper and perhaps to write a novel based on his experiences.

Lewis urged his brother Claude to accompany him on the expedition, since Claude had always relished rugged outdoor activities. He also attempted to persuade Charles Brigham, dentist Charles Miner, and other St. Cloud residents to join them, but to no avail.[4] Ultimately the party consisted of Harry and Claude Lewis; Paymaster Magistrate W. R. Taylor of Regina, Saskatchewan; Dr. A. J. MacFadyen, also of Regina; and eight Indian canoe bearers.[5]

The Lewises took the train to Winnipeg, where they met Indian Commissioner W. R. Graham June 6. They were greeted by the secretary of the Winnipeg Kiwanis Club and a photographer from the newspaper. Thirty minutes after the brothers were settled in their hotel, reporters appeared for interviews. Harry dazzled them by volunteering everything they wanted to hear.

When Lewis was asked what he wanted to see first, he replied that he had always wanted to behold the government liquor house. Two bottles of scotch were provided, and Lewis was introduced to the assembled officials, all of whom were familiar with his reputation as a major author.

At the Fort Garry Hotel, where a luncheon was held, the president of the Kiwanis Club presented Lewis to a filled house of nearly four hundred people. The author delivered a lecture on Anglo-American relations that was well received.

The Lewises met with Commissioner Graham, who had served as an Indian agent in southern Saskatchewan for twenty-eight years. Graham had witnessed the growth of Winnipeg from a town of just four hundred people to a bustling metropolis of more than two hundred thousand. Graham and his wife were excellent hosts and saw to it that their visitors saw everything they desired before leaving by rail to Regina. Lewis was so popular in Winnipeg that their departure for Prince Albert was delayed so that the curious could catch a glimpse of him.

In Prince Albert, the brothers met Chief Magistrate Taylor. As they awaited the appearance of the doctor who would accompany them on the expedition, a young man walked in and gave Taylor a letter. In reading it, the magistrate roared heartily, for the intruder was none other than A. J. MacFadyen, the expedition's physician. "Mac," as he was called, had been out of medical school but a couple of years.

That newspapers had fully carried the story of Sinclair Lewis's treaty expedition caused the writer no little concern, since one article had mentioned that they carried twenty thousand dollars with which to pay each Indian five dollars for what had once been Indian land. The money was to be carried in the express section of the train. As far as Big River and the end of the rail line, the express company was responsible for the money. After that, once the first canoe touched water, fiscal responsibility was shifted to the party itself.

Lewis and company finally set out across Crooked Lake (Cowan Lake) in a drizzle at 2:30 in the afternoon, with a strong north wind against them. There were four canoes in the party, with a white man and two guides in each. By 4:00 P.M., after they had progressed twelve miles across the lake, the rain grew worse, and the party camped for supper.

Lewis was amazed at how quickly the Indians could put up camp and cook supper. Only one Indian spoke English fluently, so the conversation among the Indians was always in Cree. The Indians prepared meals and brought them to the main tent.

After traversing Crooked Lake, two of the canoes proceeded down the Cowan River one mile to a dam constructed by a lumber company to raise the lake so logs could be floated down river. The two remaining canoes, bearing Lewis and MacFadyen, had traveled to the tip of the lake before their occupants realized they had been separated from their companions. Two Indians were dispatched in pursuit and located them already on the river. Once again the party was on the right course.

The Indians shot five ducks, and the explorers had a delightful dinner. The Lewises were surprised to discover that the Indians, who had paddled all day, never seemed tired and were cheerful and easy to get along with.

Claude Lewis compared the size of the Cowan River to that of the Sauk River back home in Sauk Centre. The water was low, and the Indians had to pole around the rocks. There was always the fear that one of the boulders suddenly would break through the bottom of a canoe. Because the Cowan River was much too low for navigation, it took the explorers thirteen hours to reach Green Lake. They descended the Beaver River and pushed on toward Isle la Crosse, arriving at the Indian camp June 24.[6] At the junction of the Cowan and Beaver rivers, they witnessed their first inhabited cabin since having left Big River.[7] The man who lived there kept a halfway house for winter freighters. Although this was the only inhabited cabin in the region, they had seen many abandoned trappers' cabins along the way.

They paused at the Lake la Plonge Mission, which was run by seven Roman Catholic priests from Ottawa and by nine Gray nuns. The clerics worked for $150 per year, paid by the Canadian government, and operated a school for some sixty pupils. The French priests spoke some English.

Where the river joined Isle la Crosse Lake, Taylor hoisted the Canadian flag and informed his companions that the flag always must fly where the Indians were to be paid. Claude and Harry were overwhelmed by the size of the post, which included the Hudson's Bay Company buildings on one side, and many Indian tents, the Catholic church, the school, and the priest's house on the other. Lewis had enjoyed much publicity since the expedition commenced, but at the Hudson's Bay post, a bishop was visiting the mission, and Lewis was merely a secondary attraction.

After compensating the Indians, the group prepared to travel to Buffalo Lake and Peter Pond Lake for delivery of more payments to various tribes. Lewis decided to wait at the mission until the group returned in a few days. The 4:00 A.M.-to-10:00 P.M. grind was beginning to tax his nerves.

Claude Lewis, Taylor, MacFadyen, and their Indian guides departed for the Buffalo River June 26, traversed Isle la Crosse Lake, and ascended Deep River into Little Buffalo Lake, Buffalo Narrows, and Big Buffalo Lake.[8] They continued up the La Loche June 29. They paid the Indians and started back to Isle la Crosse July 1.

When Lewis rejoined the group after a much-needed respite, the four canoes traversed the north arm of Isle la Crosse Lake and entered the Churchill River, riding the river to the Snake Rapids. Forced to abandon the comfort of the Churchill, where they had enjoyed the privilege of their motors, they traveled through a series of lakes, tiny streams, and portages and arrived at Lac la Ronge July 14.

At la Ronge they found an Episcopal mission, and for Harry and Claude, it was like being home among Protestants again.[9] It proved to be an oasis, and the brothers were relieved to find that there was monthly mail service between the outpost and the outside world. By now, Lewis was longing to return to civilzation, and the little bit of it which had been vouchsafed him turned his thoughts even more in that direction.

Continuing north across Lac la Ronge for forty miles, they then struggled through four portages and were again on the Churchill River a few miles west of Stanley, and arrived there July 17.[10] In the wilderness between the Episcopal mission and Stanley, Lewis told Taylor he had had enough of the trip.[11] He said he planned to leave the party at Pelican Narrows and go by way of Sturgeon Landing to Cumberland House and then by steamer to Le Pas. He was completely worn out and was finding it impossible to keep up. Claude, nonetheless, considered the trip good therapy for his brother, for he was away from long, tedious hours of writing and, more important, was finally free of alcohol.

Harry's mind was made up, however, and Claude, as much as he wanted to keep going, informed his brother that he would leave with him. Knowing that Claude wished to see the beautiful Reindeer Lake country, Harry insisted that they separate.

Claude permitted his brother to return with two of the Indians, one of the rough tents, and the food they required. It was only a three-day trip to Cumberland House via the Saskatchewan River, and the trip would be an easy one.

Lewis departed for Sturgeon Landing July 20 and caught a steamer four days later. He arrived in Le Pas on the following day and booked passage on a sleeper to Winnipeg that same evening. After spending Sunday and Monday in Winnipeg, he took a train to Sauk Centre, where he arrived July 29.

After Lewis deserted the party, Claude, MacFadyen, Taylor, and the six Indians completed the journey, which took them down the Churchill River to the junction of the Reindeer River and into Reindeer Lake, whence they proceeded north across the lake, arriving in Du Brochet July 29.[12] Du Brochet lies just south of the fifty-eighth parallel and was the northernmost point they reached on the trip. Returning to a point only thirty miles from the southern end of Reindeer Lake, they proceeded down the Rabbit River into Rabbit Lake, subsequently making portages into Hunting Lake, Loon Lake, Loon River, and the Churchill River to Pukitawakun, which they reached August 6. Between Reindeer Lake and Pukitawakun, they had made twenty-three portages. Returning to the Churchill for a day, they paddled to Duck Lake. After nineteen more portages, they reached Pelican Lake August 12. Traversing Pelican and Beaver lakes to the Sturgeon River, Sturgeon Lake, and Cumberland Lake, they reached the Saskatchewan River, where they boarded a steamer for Le Pas, arriving there August 20. They reached Prince Albert by rail August 23.

A year after the expedition, Harry wrote Claude and acknowledged receipt of his diary, which he had found stimulating and had decided to use as an outline for a novel about the Canadian wilderness, which he intended to call *Mantrap*.[13] He insisted that Claude organize, type, and bind the manuscript as a permanent record of the expedition.

In *Mantrap*, Lewis chronicles a train ride with Indian Commissioner W. R. Graham, extending to Graham the fictitious role of a sergeant in the Royal Canadian Mounted Police.[14] The sergeant tells a frightened Ralph Prescott (Sinclair Lewis) of an experienced waterman who attempted to shoot Singing Rapids. His body, most likely dashed upon the rocks, had never been found, although a piece of the canoe and a single paddle turned up. Prescott realizes that he is a coward and is terrified by the rapids and all the unknown risks of the wilderness. (Graham presumably had forewarned Lewis of the dangers he might expect, and it is likely that Lewis, like Prescott, was frightened, for he was not an experienced canoeist or swimmer; splashing about in Sauk Centre's placid Hoboken Creek was nothing compared to the struggle to stay alive in dangerous rapids.)

Lewis's description of Whitewater in *Mantrap* parallels the description of Big River in Claude Lewis's diary. Both towns lie at the edge of the frontier. Claude Lewis wrote in his diary June 24, 1924:

> Big River is an abandoned sawmill town, now of about 200 people and four years ago had 1500. The big sawmill is being

torn down. All the decent timber in the region of Cowan Lake
has been cut. Now the town lives at the end of the railway, a
shipping point for the whitefish industry of the Northern
Lakes, and as the point for carrying in goods during the
winter. The town is much more active in winter than in summer. All the freight is taken in during the winter. The Hudson Bay Company do not ship by water in this country as I
had suspected, but ship all by sled, and carry out fur on the
return trip.

Lewis's description of the fictional hamlet of Whitewater is similar:

Whitewater was once a sawmill town of fifteen hundred persons. But the patriotic lumber company has slashed away all
the timber, that is, all the timber that was not carelessly
burned, and the place has dwindled to a hundred souls—a
cluster of tumbling shanties in a prickly wilderness of stumps
and bogs.

The chief adornment is a tall iron sawmill chimney, covered with a dome of wire netting to keep in the sparks. But
the chimney is ruined now and likely to collapse in the next
storm. The secondary pride of Whitewater, rising loftily
among the tar-paper shanties, is the Bunger House: Meals
and Lodging.[15]

The Bunger House may not have been authentic, but at least there
was a place similar to it, and an argument did occur, although the
circumstances were altered in the novel. When Harry and Claude
went down to breakfast, the cook rushed out and verbally assaulted
them for failing to pay for their supper the previous evening. Harry
assured the irate cook that they had paid at the hotel desk, and they
went to find the desk clerk for verification. An argument ensued
because the desk clerk operated the pool tables, liquors and rooms, but
it was the cook who collected for the meals. There were no signs
posted requesting separate payment. The Lewises departed in favor
of a private place, and upon leaving the "Bunger House," they
notified the management that they were going out for a "clean"
breakfast.

In *Mantrap*, a grimy Bert Bunger refuses to serve Prescott and his
companion, Woodbury, and boldly tells them that supper was over at
6:40.[16] The hungry travelers insist that they never were summoned,
and Bunger replies that they are simply too lazy to come to supper.
Prescott and Woodbury demand that the cook prepare something for
them, but Bunger holds his ground. The argument quickly swells,

and Bunger demands immediate payment for the room. The two protagonists leave to have their Indians cook them some bacon. Again, they are treated to another "clean"-meal.

The first hundred pages of Claude Lewis's diary parallel fairly accurately events in the first half of *Mantrap*. It is only in the second half of the novel that the fiction begins. Throughout *Mantrap*, Lewis utilizes genuine incidents from their canoe trip to make the novel believable. An inexperienced Sinclair Lewis, for instance, brought along too much luggage for the Indians to carry or to load in a canoe; Prescott does the same thing. For both Lewis and Prescott, it was their first trip into the Canadian wilderness. Lewis had spent a week at a lumber camp in Cass Lake, but the camp had been a civilized one, and it didn't matter how much luggage he toted. Ralph Prescott's most hair-raising ordeal before his trip had been a grueling game of chess.

Both Lewis and Prescott were shocked to find that Indians looked far different than they had envisioned. They had been prepared to discover primitive natives garbed in traditional clothing; instead, they found red men who wore white men's clothing and used outboard motors on their canoes. They also were surprised to find that one of the Indians spoke fluent English and to discover that they were hard workers and loyal companions.

In *Mantrap*, Lewis incorporates descriptions of streams, portages, settlements, and the manner in which canoes were handled. Even the poker games that were played in makeshift camps are recounted in the novel.

Lewis was anything but an experienced woodsman; throughout Claude Lewis's diary, there appear references to Harry's resting while other members of the expedition were hard at work. Lewis continues to reflect his own disenchantment through Ralph Prescott: "He became a serf to Crees and to Woodbury, with little thought, small feeling and only a numb sense of his own stupidity—an insignificant figure crawling over the giant lakes, amid the engulfing gloom of forests." [17]

Lewis held a distinct advantage over Prescott because he was fond of his traveling companion, Claude; but neither Prescott nor anyone else could be fond of boisterous Wes Woodbury, who is described by Lewis as a "large and juicy drumstick from the fricasseed chicken at Sunday dinner" whose "laughter had all the horror of gears jammed by an unskilled driver." [18] Though Lewis and Prescott both wanted their companions to believe they could handle the wilderness, both were forced to flee—Prescott from Joe Easter after he had stolen his wife, and Lewis from the rigors of camp life.

Lewis assured Claude, Taylor, and MacFadyen that they were not

characters in his novel and that he was only borrowing the experience
for his book. In a letter to Claude dated July 22, 1925, Lewis reiterated
this decision:

> Thank you for your telegram. I shall await the blank for
> Freeman, and your notes on Canada, for which I shall be
> extremely grateful. I want to look them over to get back into
> my mind some of the atmosphere of N. Saskatchewan (tho
> said mind is still reasonably filled with said atmosphere any-
> way!) because I'm going to write a magazine serial story laid in
> that country. Do not be afraid that I'll use any of the stuff in
> an embarrassing way, because I'm going to be careful not to
> use any real people as characters in the story. In fact I'm
> going to invent a whole new region up there—supposed to be
> laid about where the Churchill River is, but with all the rivers,
> Hudson Bay posts, lakes, etc., given entirely fictitious names.
> The story will be about 60,000 words long—only a third of the
> length of Arrowsmith—and will appear either in the Cosmo-
> politan, Red Book, or Designer.

In a letter to his father dated July 22, 1925, Lewis referred to the
novel as "Mantrap Lake." In another, to Claude Lewis, dated October
24, 1925, he had dropped the *Lake*. He announced that the novel had
been accepted by *Collier's Weekly* and would run for twelve install-
ments. Lewis was paid $42,500 for his efforts. In the same letter, he
reassured Claude that none of the crew were described. He complained of the "fool tendency" in humans to identify with fictional
characters, and he seemed intent on reassuring his brother that he
was not the dreadful Wes Woodbury. Lewis asked Claude to write
Taylor and MacFadyen to reassure them that they were not characters in the story.

Lewis, however, never denied that he was Ralph Prescott. The guilt
Prescott experiences in thinking of Woodbury scampering through
the uncharted wilderness alone is authentic. Lewis, too, felt remorse
at having left his companions.

Lewis glorified his own actions by creating his own ending (the
fictitious second half of the novel). Ralph Prescott comes to the wilderness, meets Joe Easter, and falls in love with his wife. In an attempt
to free her from the tedious routine of the wilderness, he escapes
with her. A chase ensues, with Prescott and the girl fleeing from responsibility.

But what was Sinclair Lewis running from? It is easy to hypothesize
that he was shirking responsibility, avoiding the hard routine of por-

tages and makeshift camps. Nonetheless, one must consider that by the time the party reached Stanley he had glimpsed enough of wilderness to write a novel.

Many of Claude Lewis's friends in St. Cloud felt Sinclair had not made the grade and had fabricated his story to save face.[19] It was, after all, Lewis's idea to accompany the expedition, and Claude, who was asked along, had to finish it for him. Yet Harry is to be given some credit for surviving the rough outing. For someone so frail and inexperienced, he faced the situation remarkably well. He achieved his goal of collecting data and added another colorful page to his own life. But although the Saskatchewan experience produced a minor novel, it also marked another failure. Like Prescott, Lewis could not endure the hardships of the north country and had to look elsewhere for peace of mind. He was fortunate that he didn't have to face an angry Wes Woodbury when he reached home.

9

Pequot Lakes

A delightful place; rather ragged and uncivilized woods shut-
ting off the world on one side and a lake opening almost like
an arm of the sea on the other with a sand beach like that of
the ocean.[1]

PUBLISHER BILLY FAWCETT, creator of "Captain Billy's Whiz Bang" joke
books, came to Minnesota's Big Pelican Lake near the town of Pequot
Lakes on a hunting and fishing expedition in 1921.[2] He was impressed
by the unspoiled wilderness, which harbored only an eight-acre
homestead with a single farmhouse. His dream of a wilderness resort
retreat quickly came true; he soon purchased the land, built his own
home, and then added additional cottages and a main lounge.

Soon after its opening, Breezy Point Lodge gained a national reputation for being the "in" place for "in" people. Plates inlaid with gold
were used daily in the supper club; the beautiful log structures were
accentuated with hunting trophies from Fawcett's numerous African
safaris; gaming tables, entertainers, and movie stars from around the
world attracted guests.

Night life during those Roaring Twenties summers were high-
lighted by the sounds of the big bands, whose music echoed across
the lake; but Captain Billy entertained so lavishly that the resort produced a profit only one year.

Robert B. Hamilton, who operated the Deauville Club Casino in
Minneapolis, accompanied Fawcett on one of his treks to Pelican
Lake.[3] Fawcett and Hamilton were good friends, and it had been
Hamilton who helped Fawcett select the property for Breezy Point.
Once the Breezy Point Lodge officially opened, Hamilton operated a
casino in the basement; this casino, the Pelican Club, eventually
moved into a separate building on the same property.

Sinclair Lewis had been in Kansas City in 1926, researching *Elmer
Gantry*.[4] On April 24, 1926, Lewis wrote his brother Claude and in-

Breezy Point Lodge. Lewis called it "the finest summer resort hotel in Minnesota." Photograph courtesy Breezy Point Lodge.

formed him that he was in the company of a Unitarian clergyman, Rev. L. M. Birkhead, who was assisting him with background data for the novel. He asked Claude, who was living in St. Cloud, to find two cabins in northern Minnesota—one cabin for Birkhead, his wife, and son Kenneth; the other for himself. Lewis continued to look on his own.

On May 26, Lewis and Birkhead lunched at Breezy Point and were introduced to Bob Hamilton.[5] Hamilton owned a summer cottage five miles up the shore of Pelican Lake and was interested in renting it for the summer. Lewis immediately took it, and it was soon occupied by the Birkhead family. Approximately one hundred yards away, two tents were erected. One served as Lewis's sleeping quarters and study; with the base constructed of wood and only the top of canvas, it proved comfortable. The remaining tent was occupied by Lewis's two Hawaiian cooks.

Lewis departed from Pequot Lakes (then known only as Pequot) May 28 but returned June 3 to take occupancy of the cottage. The Birkheads joined him one week later. Lewis made good use of the week by working furiously on *Elmer Gantry*. Reporters from the *Minneapolis Tribune* came to the cottage to interview him and take pictures. The result was an article entitled "Sinclair Lewis, Nature's Own, Roughs It."[6] After his failure in Saskatchewan two years before, he probably relished an article that dispelled any notions that he couldn't handle the wilderness.

Lewis may have retreated from the outside world during the summer of 1926, but the world—or at least Minnesota—was reluctant to forget him.[7] The local sheriff, a notorious bootlegger, sold most of his illegal product to guests at the hotel, and whenever they assembled, Lewis was among the thirsty. William McNally, vice-president of the *Minneapolis Tribune,* visited him and recorded the experience in an article for *The Nation* a year later. Karl Andrist, a young violinist from Minneapolis, came to visit him, and Lewis, regarding the musician as a neglected genius, let him borrow his car and then gave him five thousand dollars to study in Europe.

Lewis was delighted to see his Minneapolis friends but was eager to greet his family as well. In a letter to Claude dated June 6, 1926, he adamantly urged his brother to bring the family to Pequot Lakes for a visit:

> I'm getting settled now, and I like the cottage very much. It's not as large as I had hoped, but it's beautifully secluded—no other house for miles. Why don't Mary and the girls and you run up for some Sunday? The place can't be over 110 miles from St. Cloud, with the roads such that you could drive it in 3½ hours. Here's the exact directions: Pequot is about 25 miles north of Brainerd, on the through highway to Walker and Cross Lake. I'm about nine miles from Pequot, on the Cross Lake Road. The cottage belongs to one R. B. Hamilton, and a sign with his name is out in front of the place. The Cross Lake road is marked all the way thru from Pequot.

In another letter to Claude, dated June 10, 1926, he acknowledged his brother's acceptance of the invitation and confirmed their plans:

> Your plans suit me fine. I know it will be a joy to Kenneth to have the girls with him for a week, and I think they will all like one another. As I understand it, Mary will spend all the week in Cass Lake, but you will have to return to St. Cloud for the week. Have I that right? We'd be awfully glad to have both of you for as long as you can stay, and I just want to get clear what the plans are so's to have enough beds out.

Lewis's reference to "getting enough beds out" was perhaps his way of informing his brother that they would be staying in the cottage with the Birkheads and not one of the small tents. Lewis liked others to believe he was roughing it in the makeshift tent; more often than not, however, he slept with the others in the cottage. He went on:

There will be no trouble about meeting Mary at Pequot if she will let us know just when she will arrive; we have two cars and four drivers in the crowd, for my Hawaiian boy proves to be able to drive perfectly well, and I send him clear down to Brainerd on errands. . . . There's only one thing which I don't know—whether I'll be able to drive up to Cass Lake with you and spend the night of Sunday 27th. That depends on who may happen to be around here for the day. But there is no need of deciding that till you get here. . . . We'll expect you, then, on Sunday 27th, some time about noon.

He attempted to interest Claude in buying property near Pequot Lakes. He said he would be talking with a couple of real estate promoters who were selling Breezy Point property and would have them stop in St. Cloud to see him the next time they were on their way to Minneapolis.

Claude and his family had no trouble in locating the Sinclair Lewis cottage and arrived on schedule.[8] The girls, especially Isabel, were interested in Kenneth Birkhead, and he seemed to reciprocate. They played with Harry's two dogs, Nymph and Triton, and frolicked on the steep little hill that led to the lake. Rickety planks that served as steps delivered the children to the sandy beach, but they raced away in terror when they accidently discovered a nest of green snakes beneath the stairway.

Lewis may have called the Pequot Lakes experience "roughing it," but to judge from the manner in which the little girls were dressed, it was anything but rough.[9] They wore frocks that had been handmade by a dressmaker and cost from thirty-five dollars to forty dollars.

Harry showed the Claude Lewises the tent where he wrote. The family was astonished to find that it housed only a table, chair, and typewriter.[10] They learned quickly that although Harry did his writing in the strange-looking tent, he actually lived with the others in the Hamilton cottage. Though he wanted everyone to believe he was roughing it in Pequot Lakes, he actually was living comfortably in a house with all the modern conveniences of the city.

One Saturday night Harry escorted Claude's wife, Mary, to the Pelican Club for a look at the gaming tables. The children, meanwhile, were carted off to a movie in Pequot Lakes. On another evening, Harry took the Claude Lewises to the Pequot Lakes movie theater to see the film version of *Mantrap*. The manager of the theater, quickly recognizing Lewis, proudly announced that the author of *Mantrap* was present and asked him to address the moviegoers. Lewis, who always had been a master in the art of ad-libbing, shocked the manager and the audience by stating he was glad he had read the book, for he would not have recognized it from the movie.[11]

The Claude Lewises noticed that the Birkheads were always nearby and ready to serve the author whenever he needed them.[12] Birkhead frequently was asked questions regarding religion, and Mrs. Birkhead served as housekeeper and gracious hostess. The Claude Lewises found the Birkheads delightful and relished their own reunion with Harry.

The visit was marred by one incident. An edgy Harry Lewis grew impatient with his Hawaiian cook, lost his temper, handed the man fifty dollars, and demanded that he leave immediately. Someone quickly drove the boy to the bus depot, sparing him the author's wrath. Lewis's conscience soon reprimanded him for his actions. "What have I done? What have I done?" he cried, breaking into tears at the dining room table. The ever-faithful Mrs. Birkhead was quick to comfort him.

The solitude of the north country, so necessary to his writing, began to bore him, and he yearned for the night life of Breezy Point. Every evening he would drop by the lodge for dinner and would emerge much later very drunk.[13] Lewis considered Breezy Point to be among the finest lodges in the entire Midwest; formal wear was required in the evenings, but Lewis was an exception to the rule. He would appear with his tie pulled sloppily aside and his shirt sleeves rolled up. James Ellwood, who worked at Breezy Point, was assigned the task of taking Lewis home each night in a pickup truck and putting him to bed.

During the last few evenings that Lewis stayed at Pequot Lakes, he avoided Breezy Point and hosted wild parties that were talked about all around the lake.[14] Guests at Breezy Point arrived at the Lewis cottage by the carload, and all departed under the influence of liquor. At approximately 11:00 P.M., Lewis, weary of the intruders, would fire a pistol to signify the end of the festivities. The next day he would refuse to see anyone and reinforced his feelings by posting No Trespassing signs on his property.

Two priests once arrived at the Lewis cottage bearing half a case of communion wine. Young Kenneth Birkhead, dispatched to locate Lewis, informed him that Upton Sinclair had arrived. Lewis galloped out of the house, took the prank in stride, and the three men proceeded to empty as many bottles as they could.

Lewis's fascination for the clergy took him to the town of Crosby, some twenty-five miles from his cottage.[15] Two little girls heard music emanating from the home of a Catholic priest. Peeking through the French doors, the girls glimpsed a ruddy-faced author conversing with a piano-playing priest, who was hammering out "The St. Louis Blues."

In August he left for a week to spend some time at a Rainy Lake island retreat with some guests from Breezy Point, but, after a death in the family and an unscheduled trip to Sauk Centre, he returned to his own retreat in Pequot Lakes. There was additional work on *Elmer Gantry*, but with the summer drawing to a close, he began making preparations to locate suitable lodgings for the fall.

In September Lewis left Pequot Lakes for good. With winter approaching, it was time for a change of scenery, and he assured himself that he had accomplished what he had set out to do: He had given substance to *Elmer Gantry*. But the guests at Breezy Point had begun to bore him, and many residents had taken a dim view of his incessant drinking. On the day of his departure, he had completed half of *Elmer Gantry* and had given the locals something to talk about.

SINCLAIR LEWIS SITES IN PEQUOT LAKES

116. Sinclair Lewis cottage (Robert Hamilton home): Big Pelican Lake.
117. Breezy Point Lodge: Big Pelican Lake.

Breezy Point Lodge. Sinclair Lewis worked on his novel Elmer Gantry here in 1926. Photograph courtesy Breezy Point Lodge.

10

Rainy Lake

My father has never forgiven me for *Main Street*. . . . When I saw him a few weeks ago, we shook hands—but he can't comprehend the book, much less grasp that it's the greatest tribute I knew how to pay him.[1]

SINCLAIR LEWIS made many friends at the Breezy Point Lodge in Pequot Lakes during the summer of 1926, but one of his most valuable associations was with wealthy mine owner B. G. Dahlberg.[2] Dahlberg owned a summer estate called Red Crest on his own private island in Rainy Lake in far northern Minnesota, and he cordially invited Lewis to the lavish retreat.

Lewis planned to spend one week at the island estate, located ten miles east of the town of Ranier, and planned to work on *Elmer Gantry*, which had taken shape at the Pequot Lakes cottage. The Pequot Lakes area had been an excellent place to write, but he had been besieged constantly by curious visitors and also was diverted by the glamorous nightlife of what he termed "Minnesota's finest summer hotel." Here on a private island in Rainy Lake, on the edge of the Minnesota-Canadian wilderness, he felt he would find the privacy he needed to fulfill his writing ambitions.

After the Dahlbergs picked up Lewis and took him to their retreat, the author was surprised and exhilarated to find his old friend Charles Breasted, with whom he had struck up a friendship in 1922.[3]

As he had done in Pequot Lakes, Lewis erected his by-now-famous tent outside the Dahlberg mansion. The teepee house was made of large poles covered with birchbark. It had a "captain's walk" around the top, large velvet cushions strategically positioned about the interior, and a fireplace in the center.[4] It was connected by telephone to the Dahlberg house. He spent his nights inside the mansion with the other guests, but his days were spent in the tent, where he worked on *Elmer Gantry*.

Lewis did not devote all his time to working and playing on the island, for he made frequent trips to the town of International Falls.[5] Eager to be accepted by the tourists who vacationed in the wilderness mecca, he signed a visitors' register at a local drugstore and chatted with patrons, not as Sinclair Lewis the famous writer, but as Sinclair Lewis the vacationer. He also indulged in some fishing on Rainy Lake and discussed the sport with such local residents as Don Johnson and Bert Lehman. Some of his most cherished discussions were with Red Crest caretaker Gilbert Carlson, whose uncanny knowledge of local history and lore fascinated him.

On the night of August 29, Lewis, secluded at Red Crest, had a premonition that word of his father's death would reach him the following morning.[6] He was so upset that he awakened Breasted and begged him to sit with him. Precisely at midnight, Dr. E. J. Lewis did in fact die. For several days before his death, a motorboat expedition had scoured local streams in an effort to locate Lewis with news of his father's steadily worsening condition.

The motorboat expedition finally reached Lewis on August 31, after a search of all the remote islands in the area. Lewis, having experienced the frightening premonition, was hardly shocked by the message; he made arrangements to leave the island at once. After driving all night back to Pequot Lakes, he and Breasted gathered what they needed and drove directly to Sauk Centre for the funeral.

Lewis had never made a habit of staying long in a single area. He had been forced in the past to leave communities because of his drinking, because of sharp differences with the wealthy, and because of ideological differences with the poor. But Rainy Lake had been a blessing to him, and he had been happy there. He had made it clear to local journalists that he had a fondness for the lake and the boundary forests.[7] Now death had forced him to take leave. With a heavy heart and a guilty conscience, he left the boundary waters forever.

SINCLAIR LEWIS SITE ON RAINY LAKE

118. B. G. Dahlberg estate: Now Musket Inn on Musket Island, ten miles east of Ranier.

11

Madison

Already today I have found a house—nearly as good as our Beverly Hills castle minus patio and pool, and just as large, at one third the rent. It's on a curving hillside road, very near the sprawling giant beehive of the university.[1]

DURING THE SUMMER OF 1940, Sinclair Lewis was coaxed by Norman Foerster, professor of American literature at the State University of Iowa, into accepting a teaching appointment there.[2] But C. A. Phillips, acting president of the university, rejected him because of his reputation as a drunkard. Lewis was outraged.

On September 14 he left New York for the Midwest, still seeking a teaching position at the University of Minnesota. He had worked hard in New York on *Felicia Speaking*, a play, and was now determined to prepare the effort for Broadway in a peaceful Midwestern environment.

His old friend Joseph Brewer, now president of Olivet College in Michigan, had written him some months earlier and offered him a teaching position there. Lewis visited the college and met with a group of young student writers who had been assembled in his honor. He found the students dull amateurs, rejected the offer, and left for the University of Minnesota.

He paused in Madison, Wisconsin, to visit his old friend, poet William Ellery Leonard, September 23. Leonard, who had come to the University of Wisconsin as an English professor in 1906, suffered from numerous psychological disorders, including acute agoraphobia, and had written a book-length autobiographical poem entitled *The Locomotive God*, which described his fears.[3] Leonard also was plagued by emotional "distance terrors" and felt insecure and confined whenever he was away from his house. A train whistle could send him fleeing toward home, and for much of his adult life he was unable to stray more than a hundred feet from his home. Leonard wrote another lengthy poem, *Two Lives*, shortly after his twenty-three-year-old wife committed suicide by swallowing poison. It was *The Locomotive God* and *Two Lives* that established Leonard's reputation as a serious poet.

Leonard arranged a luncheon for Lewis with members of the university's English department and a dinner with its president, Clarence A. Dykstra.[4] Lewis was introduced to Merritt Y. Hughes, chairman of the English department, and the two discussed the feasibility of Lewis's presiding over a class in creative writing.[5] Lewis wished to be in residence for three to four months (roughly one semester) and offered to work without salary as an English lecturer.

It was subsequently arranged for Reginald Watters, a graduate student, and his wife, Primrose, to guide Lewis on a tour of the campus.[6] The author treated a group of selected students to dinner, and after the meal, there was a reception in the Watters' home. A game was played in which each person pretended to have entered a lecture late and then would be required to guess what the speaker was talking about. Lewis was magnificent.

Clarence A. Dykstra Residence; 130 North Prospect Avenue, Madison. As president of the University of Wisconsin, he signed Lewis to a teaching contract. Photograph by R. Alain Everts, 1981.

The next day he departed for Minneapolis to inspect the University of Minnesota. Haunted by the size of the city, however, he quickly decided against accepting an appointment there. He finally took a job at the University of Wisconsin, lured to Madison by its more comfortable size—just more than sixty thousand people. He also was impressed by the domed capitol at one end of town, the university's towers at the other, and by the green parkland between two beautiful lakes. He recalled having been in Madison on January 16, 1939, when he appeared in a performance of his play, *Angela Is Twenty-Two*: In spite of the negative reviews, he had grown fond of the city even then. He now decided to settle in Madison.

Lewis was led to an elegant residential neighborhood known as University Heights and shown a mansion at 1712 Summit Avenue, which was at that time occupied by a widow, Mrs. Charles H. Johnson.[7] He liked the house and rented it on September 30, 1940.[8] The house, perched on a high hill called Breezy Terrace, had been constructed in 1927 by W. F. Sloane, a Chicago engineer, and had been sold in 1930 to Mr. and Mrs. Johnson, the former a student at the University of Wisconsin. Mrs. Johnson suffered from a heart condition, so an elevator had been installed within the house to give

Sinclair Lewis house, 1712 Summit Avenue, Madison, Wisconsin. Lewis rented the spacious mansion, complete with elevator on September 30, 1940. In this house he worked on his play Felicia Speaking. Photograph by R. Alain Everts, 1981.

her mobility; it was the only one of its kind in Madison. From the upper floors she could catch a glimpse of every lake in the city.

Lewis was able to rent the dwelling because Charles Johnson had recently passed away, and real estate agent Whitford L. Huff had convinced Mrs. Johnson that Lewis would make a suitable tenant. Mrs. Johnson was only mildly interested, but Huff persisted, arguing that Lewis would pay handsomely. Mrs. Johnson's attorney felt that since Lewis was certainly reliable, she should lease the home, and he urged her to take a trip. This she did, and when she returned, her attorney greeted her with the news that her spacious home had been rented to novelist Sinclair Lewis.

Lewis brought with him his ever-faithful chauffeur, Joseph Hardrick, and a housekeeper. Mrs. Johnson immediately resented her new tenant because of the menagerie of cats he brought with him. Lewis always had been fond of animals and had purchased the cats as companions, since he had separated from Dorothy Thompson and needed the animals' companionship.

Lewis was within easy walking distance of the school but still far enough away to be assured of some privacy. He considered himself lucky to occupy such an opulent residence.

Lewis complained to fellow instructor Harry Hayden Clark that he was weary of secretaries who knew nothing about publishing, and Clark suggested Primrose Watters, since she once had been employed by a publishing house in London.[9] She was interviewed for a secretarial position and hired immediately.[10] Primrose's husband, Reginald, worshiped Lewis and considered his association with the author to be among the highlights of his life.[11]

Primrose Watters would arrive at the Lewis house every morning, stay through lunch, and then leave during the afternoon.[12] On one occasion, she accidently ignored the Do Not Disturb sign posted on the author's door to inform him of a long-distance telephone call; an angry Lewis, garbed in a tattered dressing gown, reprimanded her by thundering that the sign meant what it said. But Lewis was very fond of her, and the misunderstanding was quickly forgotten.

Everyone was eager to interview the celebrated author, and Lewis was eager to talk about Wisconsin. He praised the undying "Wisconsin spirit" and professed admiration for such Wisconsin writers as Zona Gale, Edna Ferber, Glenway Wescott, August Derleth, Edward Heth, and Mark Schorer.

At a reception held at the home of Merritt Hughes, with President Clarence Dykstra present, Lewis met the school's staff but became furious when one of the regents commented that he would rather have Dorothy Thompson at the university than have Sinclair Lewis.[13] Lewis threatened to resign, but the embarrassed dignitaries, especially Merritt Hughes, persuaded him to retain his position.

Hughes's guests quickly discovered that Sinclair Lewis was less thunder and lightning than he was shy and introverted. When the author was introduced to Prof. Robert B. Doremus, he remarked to a colleague, "I wonder if he's as scared as I am."[14]

Some faculty members greeted Lewis cooly. They surmised that he was taking notes on them that would later appear in a novel. Lewis, who had always considered Midwesterners provincial, reassured them he was there only because he wanted to be.

Harry Hayden Clark also hosted a dinner party for Lewis, to which he invited sixteen scholars from various departments.[15] As Lewis left the party, one woman shouted after him, "Now don't write a book and put us all in it." It seemed he never would be forgiven for having written *Main Street*.

When Lewis attended an English department faculty tea, Clark introduced him to Prof. Ellsworth Barnard.[16] In an effort to make Lewis feel at home, Clark nodded at Barnard and quipped, "He's new here, too." Lewis was greatly amused by this simple gesture, perhaps because he saw in Barnard someone else on public display.

Prof. Samuel Rogers did not seek an introduction to Lewis because he knew the author was a distinguished guest of the university, and Rogers did not want to bother him.[17] At the University Theater, Lewis recognized Rogers, scolded him for not coming to visit and proceeded to invite him to dinner. It soon became apparent to Rogers, as well as to others on campus, that, despite his reputation, Lewis was not drinking during his stay in Madison.

Rogers, who taught French at the university, was also a writer of merit, and Lewis was quick to praise his *Dusk at the Grove*, which had won a prize from the *Atlantic Monthly*.[18] Lewis was, however, less than complimentary about Rogers' latest novel, *Lucifer in Pine Lake*, and blue-penciled a copy of it before he returned it to the author. Rogers, although displeased by the gesture, was convinced Lewis meant well and took no offense.

Lewis devoted little time to his colleagues, but he did strike up friendships with John Steuart Curry, the artist in residence at the university, and Gunnar Johansen, a gifted pianist. Lewis told Johansen, whom he met at the home of the school's music director, that he wished to learn to play the piano.[19] When Lewis rented a Steinway, Johansen became his mentor and came to the Summit mansion once a week for six weeks to teach the author the keyboard.

Johansen was impressed by what he considered Lewis's most striking feature, his indomitable spirit. He took an instant liking to Lewis and found him to be much more sociable than scholarly.

Lewis made very little progress on the piano, and Johansen came to realize that the author was attempting to steady his hands by taking piano lessons. The tremor was obvious to everyone by now, but not even his closest associates commented upon it.

Lewis and Johansen frequently went for long rides in the country in Lewis's capacious Buick roadster. They would drive to the end of Mineral Point Road beyond Pine Bluff because Lewis was fond of the territory. When the destination was reached, Johansen could always expect Lewis to exclaim, "Oh, can't you see a house here. Can't you see a house here?" On one occasion Lewis remarked that it was the first time since he had arrived in Madison that he had wanted to stay anywhere longer than six weeks.

Most of Lewis's better writing was behind him, but students were quick to enroll in his class, one that Lewis hoped would be limited to fifteen. His latest novel, *Bethel Merriday*, had been published earlier in the year, but it had been five years since one of his books, *It Can't Happen Here*, had made any kind of impact.

Not everyone was eligible to take Lewis's class.[20] Interested applicants had one evening to compose a manuscript and deliver it to the English department. Lewis then read the manuscripts and selected the students whom he desired to participate.

Twenty-four students were finally enrolled in the class, which met Wednesdays from 4:30 to 6:00 P.M. at 354 Bascom Hall (as well as evenings by appointment in the author's residence).[21] In the classroom he was not particularly articulate.[22] He would outline a make-believe novel to which all students contributed parts of the plot.[23] The story was set in Wisconsin and dealt with the game of curling.

One student asked Lewis for his opinion of Henry Fielding's novel, *Tom Jones*; the author replied that if he had ever read it, he couldn't remember anything about it. He added that no one should like Fielding anyway. Students were shocked to learn that their instructor, a celebrated novelist, could teach a class on the novel and take a negative view of classics he may never have read.

Lewis took the time to renew his association with popular Wisconsin writer August Derleth. Derleth had long been an admirer of the older author; in 1938 he had written him and expressed his intention of dedicating a book to him. Lewis persuaded Derleth to drop the idea, since he considered himself to be a chief object of hatred within the entire left wing of literature. He attempted to convince Derleth that any linking of their names would quickly bring about the younger writer's "self-annihilation."[24]

Lewis wrote Derleth on October 18, 1940, thanked him for a copy of his latest book, *Country Growth*, and informed him that he intended to visit him at his home in nearby Sauk City.[25] Lewis always had taken an interest in young Midwestern authors, and Derleth, then only thirty-one, had already published twenty books.[26]

That same month, Lewis's friend Marcella Powers, who had been denied a role in a New York stage play, came to Madison to visit him.[27] Lewis persuaded the director of the University Theater to produce his play *Stage Door* and to give Miss Powers the role of Bernice Niemeyer.

During the first week of November, Lewis was at the home of fellow professor Henry Pochman when he received a telephone call from Dorothy Thompson, who was soon to have dinner with President and Mrs. Franklin Roosevelt.[28] Lewis suddenly became jealous of his journalist wife and informed the Pochmans that he had to return to Washington to confer with his publisher. Later that same evening, Lewis telephoned his secretary, Mrs. Watters, and requested that she come to his house prepared to work for a couple of hours.

In the morning, Lewis informed his stunned class that he was leaving the university. Addressing his loyal charges for but a few moments, he stated, "I've told you all I know about creative writing, so we might just as well stop."[29]

Members of the English department were furious; Lewis had taught only thirty-nine days and had not fulfilled his obligation.[30] Students, too, were disgusted with his conduct; members of his class issued a public manifesto stating that newspapermen had hounded them for inside information on the class and its instructor but that Lewis had extracted a promise from each of them to give no stories to the media, lest the course become a circus.

Rumors about the writer's sudden departure circulated throughout the campus. Some students felt his repulsive skin disorder had grown worse and that he had been forced to be nearer his New York doctor.[31] Many students believed he was jealous of his wife and longed to attend the presidential dinner.[32]

Lewis explained to one of his colleagues that though he taught writing, he really knew nothing about teaching.[33] He stated that he was both mentally and physically exhausted, that no one in the class was capable of good ideas, and that none could write in the first place.

Paul Fulcher, who shared an office with Prof. Robert B. Doremus, said that Lewis's departure was understandable.[34] He had finished the most rewarding aspect of the class, the teaching of creative writing, and now all that remained was the difficult part, the reading of all the long creative works.

Lewis informed his friend Gunnar Johansen that he was leaving to honor a commitment to President Roosevelt by delivering an election speech in his behalf.[35] Before leaving, Lewis asked Johansen what he owed him for his services. "You are a dollar-a-year man [one who gave his services for nothing]," Johansen replied. "According to that you would owe me just a few cents." In return, Lewis presented him with signed copies of all his books; he inscribed *Arrowsmith* "to the Dr. Gottlieb of my musical education."

Before Lewis left Madison, he asked the Watters to live rent-free in his mansion for the remainder of the semester.[36] The Watters were living in a small house on Johnson Street, and they welcomed this opportunity to move into one of Madison's most elegant homes.

The local newspapers were far from sympathetic with Lewis.[37] The *Madison State Journal* published an unflattering article entitled "We Break the Lewis Lance" November 7, 1940. The story was rebutted by Merritt Y. Hughes in an article for the same paper; it conveyed all that Lewis had done for the university and was intended to take the sting out of provincialism.

When Lewis left Madison November 7, he had broken his commitments to both his landlord and the university. He never again would be welcome in Madison. Lewis insisted that his chauffeur, Joseph Hardrick, stay in Madison for a few days to see if anything uncomplimentary was written about Lewis in the newspapers.[38] After a few days, Lewis telephoned Hardrick and summoned him to Chicago.

SINCLAIR LEWIS SITES IN MADISON

119. Sinclair Lewis residence: 1712 Summit Avenue.
120. Sinclair Lewis classroom: 354 Bascom Hall, University of Wisconsin.
121. William Ellery Leonard residence: 433 Murray (razed).
122. John Steuart Curry residence: Rural Delivery 3, Hilltop Ranch on Seminole Highway.
123. John Steuart Curry studio: 432 Lorch.
124. Samuel Rogers residence: 2121 Adams Street.
125. Clarence A. Dykstra residence: 130 North Prospect Avenue.
126. Merritt Y. Hughes residence: 150 North Prospect Avenue.
127. Reginald Watters residence: 612½ Johnson Street, number 4.

12

Excelsior

It is an oldish house, both roomy and comfortable, with a vast
porch, on which I'll dine, against the hot weather. It's on the
water, and I'll be popping into the water often—which one
does if he doesn't have to jump into the car and go some-
where. I already know from old days, quite a lot of people on
the lake, which is so huge, and has such irregular shoreline
outlines that it is supposed to have over 300 miles of shoreline.
I'll meet as many new people as I want.[1]

DURING THE SPRING of 1942, when he was living out East, Sinclair
Lewis was eager to prove that an author who had always been on the
periphery of society could go home whenever he chose. He did not,
however, wish to subject himself to a summer in torrid Minneapolis,
and, after consulting with numerous real estate agents, he began
searching for a comfortable residence in the Minnesota communities
of St. Cloud, Marine-on-St. Croix, Northfield, Faribault, and Lake
Minnetonka.

Residence in St. Cloud would have reunited him with his brother
Claude, but it was a long drive from Minneapolis, and since he was
toying with the idea of obtaining a teaching position at the University
of Minnesota, it was simply impractical to commute each day. Marine-
on-St. Croix was a quaint community reminiscent of New England,
and it was close to Taylors Falls, among Lewis's favorite areas, but it,
too, was remote. He finally settled on Lake Minnetonka. He located a
spacious house built in 1877 and situated on the shores of Lake Minnetonka, just six miles from Excelsior. The house on Edgewood Road
provided him with relief from the heat and with the solitude his work
demanded.

Lewis went to work immediately on his new novel, *Gideon Planish*,
but he took time out for excursions in every conceivable direction and
to deliver a lecture at Hamline University in St. Paul. He lectured in

114

his hometown of Sauk Centre and visited a few remaining old friends he had there; he left town convinced that the younger generation, unlike its stuffy predecessor, understood him.

At a party in Minneapolis, he was asked why he had come home after so many years, and he attempted to convince his friends, and himself, that it was a matter of roots. Minnesota had always been his home and that of his parents and grandparents. Having convinced himself of his ancestral allegiance, he departed the following morning for Elysian to record headstone inscriptions from the graves of his paternal grandparents.

Most of his time was devoted to *Gideon Planish*, and the work kept him from friends in the city who might think he wanted to party.[2]

As he had done so frequently in the past, Lewis hired a young research assistant, Donald Hart, to assist with some of the footwork for the novel.[3] Hart occupied a much smaller dwelling on the edge of the property, where he, too, could have privacy. There were so many towering shade trees on the property that Lewis, whenever he so chose, could write outside and still be sheltered from the road; the estate was eventually named Tall Trees.[4]

Gideon Planish had nothing to do with Minnesota, although it was written near Lake Minnetonka's Gideon Bay. That Lewis intended to inject some of Minnesota's local heritage into the book was evidenced by the title's relationship to the Minnetonka region's history: Peter Gideon, Ohio horticulturalist, came to the shores of Lake Minnetonka in the early 1850s, carrying apple seeds and seedlings, peach seeds, and small plum, cherry, and pear trees.[5] He converted the region into a pioneer experiment station, demonstrating that apples could be grown in Minnesota. Another Minnesota pioneer, Gideon Pond, established a mission at Oak Grove in the Minnesota River valley.[6]

As Lewis incorporated his knowledge of Minnesota history into *Gideon Planish*, the desire burned within him to tackle Minnesota writing projects. For the first time since the publication of *Main Street* in 1920, he was rereading his own novel very meticulously.[7] With the war raging in Europe and Asia, Lewis had promised the War Savings Staff of the Treasury Department that he would write a radio script entitled "Main Street Goes to War," a fictionalized account of a mobilized Gopher Prairie. The script was completed but was never produced. When Lewis wrote the Treasury Department the following March and asked why the script had never been aired, he was told that the department had never received it.

On June 3, Marcella Powers and her mother arrived to spend ten days with Lewis. For a glorious ten days, he was spared the terrible loneliness that had plagued him, and he presented the Powers to all the "right" people: the Pillsburys, William McNally, John Cowles, the F. Peavey Heffelfingers, the Addison Lewises, Alfred and Fefa Wilson, and other friends. He also introduced the Powers to his niece Virginia and her friend Dorothy Bennett, who were Marcella's own age.[8] The Powers departed from Minneapolis on June 12, for Marcella was playing in summer stock.

On June 23, Lewis began searching for a winter home in Minneapolis.[9] He disliked the city and most of his acquaintances there, but winter would make it next to impossible to remain at the lake, and he still coveted a teaching position at the University of Minnesota.

The Old Log Theater in Excelsior had originated in 1939 as a communal living experiment.[10] In 1940 the investors leased land and opened the theater with a production of *Penny Wise*. During the summer of 1942, the Old Log Theater presented a production of *Pursuit of Happiness*. For two or three weeks before the opening, there came such a steady deluge of rain, causing considerable flood damage to waterfront property in the low-lying areas, that there was much doubt that the theater could open at all. The owners, however, vowed to open on schedule and made every effort to refurbish the theater in time for the opening performance. One day, a tall, slender figure appeared at the box office and was immediately recognized as author Sinclair Lewis. He took one look at the flood within the theater and commented, "You can't open here. You're supposed to open in a few days, aren't you? It's obvious you can't open."

He suggested that they procure temporary quarters in the Excelsior Elementary School, but Bob Aden, managing director of the Old Log, insisted that the theater would open on schedule. A bet was immediately waged between Aden and Lewis. Should the theater not open on schedule, Lewis would win a pair of season tickets; should Lewis lose the wager, he would be required to take everyone in the company to Bacon Drug Store for sodas.

Aden outdid himself. Yards of gravel were poured inside the theater where pools of water stood; planks were hauled in to bridge the lakelets that had formed in the auditorium. The ;ood remained within the theater, but people were able to walk on the gravel, and those seated in the front section could keep their feet dry by resting them on the elevated planks.

The play opened on schedule; Aden was victorious. Lewis was surprised but was only too happy to treat the entire crew to sodas at Bacon Drug.

Lewis saw much of Aden and his staff during that summer. When Lewis was invited to a faculty tea at the University of Minnesota, he brought Aden and a friend, Debra Tighe, with him, as representatives of the Old Log Theater. Since Lewis was a guest himself, it was taboo for him to invite others; but he did so nonetheless to the chagrin of some faculty members.

At the tea, Lewis chided faculty members for not supporting the Old Log Theater and informed them that he considered it one of the premier playhouses in the state and that he was shocked that professional people weren't more familiar with it. When one woman congratulated Lewis for his recent novel, *Bethel Merriday*, which she had enjoyed immensely, Aden asked Lewis how anyone could thank him for that particular book when he had also written *Arrowsmith*, which Aden considered the greatest of American novels. Insulted, Lewis bellowed, "And what's wrong with *Bethel Merriday?*" Aden explained that there was nothing wrong with the novel but that it could hardly measure up to *Arrowsmith*. But it was much too late for an explanation; Lewis's pride had been wounded, and he refused to talk to Aden and Tighe for the rest of the evening. Since the two were acquainted with no one in the room and were unpopular for attending in the first place, they both were embarrassed during the remainder of the tea. It took Lewis several days to cool off, and it was not until two weeks had passed that he consented to talk to them again. *Bethel Merriday* was never discussed again.

Lewis soon resumed his visits to the Old Log, where he frequently conducted fireside chats with Aden; when the managing director suggested that the theater produce *Dodsworth*, Lewis made it clear that he considered *Angela Is Twenty-Two*, the play he had written for Marcella Powers, more appropriate. (*Angela* had opened elsewhere in the Twin Cities in January 1939 with Miss Powers performing the lead role and Lewis playing Dr. Jarrett; after three years, the play was still on tour.)

Aden liked *Angela* but felt that *Dodsworth* was a more suitable production. With no argument, Lewis yanked the *Angela* manuscript from Aden's hands, stalked out the door, and never returned to the Old Log again. The theater never produced a Sinclair Lewis play.

The following year, a much-weathered Lewis, whose misshapen teeth and speech defect now seemed more apparent, telephoned Aden while the two were in New York and invited him to a party. Aden accepted. In recalling his disagreement with Aden, Lewis soon conceded to his visitor that he had had to write a few books for money and that some were therefore inferior to others. The two reconciled and all past incidents were forgotten. The Lewis-Aden incident was unique: Usually Lewis would forever terminate an association after an argument. Perhaps Lewis realized that there was some truth in Aden's comments and that an author, even if he *had* won the Nobel Prize, was capable of writing some books that failed to match the quality of others.

Excelsior was not dependent on Minneapolis, and Lewis found everything he needed right in his own community. Like everyone else in wartime, he was required to register for his ration stamps, and his chauffeur, Joseph Hardrick, would drive him to the nearby Minnewashta Elementary School to pick up his coupons with little loss to *Gideon Planish.*[11]

When Joseph was ordered to report for a physical examination for military service that summer, he did so at the office of Dr. Stuart Lane Arey, the local draft examiner in Excelsior.[12] During the course of the examination, Hardrick informed the physician that he was employed by the famous author, Sinclair Lewis. By coincidence, Arey had attended Culver College with Lewis's nephew, Freeman Lewis. Joseph invited Arey to visit the Lewis house and meet the author, but Arey, not eager to detain a famous man from serious business, declined the invitation.

The next day, as Arey's wife was working in her garden, a limousine pulled up and out stepped Sinclair Lewis, intent upon paying the doctor a visit. When Mrs. Arey informed the author that her husband was out, Lewis invited them to his home for dinner. Dr. Arey returned later, and his wife conveyed the message, stating, "We just had a visit from the homeliest man I have ever seen." The Areys soon had dinner at the Lewis mansion, where they found their host charming and cynical. Lewis related that his father had been a country doctor and would frequently be gone for hours, only to come home, bathe, and then depart for another eighteen-hour session. "For love of humanity?" Arey asked. "Hell, no," Lewis snapped. "He did it because he had to make a living."

Lewis was growing weary of Excelsior, but he hosted one final party before settling down to house hunting and *Gideon Planish.* His niece Virginia came out to the lake for a visit, bringing with her old friends Faubion Bowers, Matt Adams, Charlie Fogg, and two Japanese boys.[13] Lewis's apparent boredom was never revealed when the next day the group was joined by Virginia's friend Dorothy Bennett, and they journeyed to the St. Croix River for an outing.

By August, however, Lewis was becoming anxious to procure a winter house in Minneapolis. The old sense of isolation was beginning to gnaw at him. For a change of pace, he took a trip to the Gateway-

Hungry Jack Lodge on northern Minnesota's Gunflint Trail, came home briefly, and then departed for the East.

On September 22, he moved into a house on Mount Curve Avenue in Minneapolis. In Excelsior, he had written much of *Gideon Planish* and had completed the radio script "Main Street Goes to War." He was satisfied with the progress he had made that summer and would soon complete his novel in Minneapolis. Little did he know that Sinclair Lewis, like the town in his radio script, now was going to war.

SINCLAIR LEWIS SITES IN EXCELSIOR

128. Sinclair Lewis residence: 26710 Edgewood Road.
129. Old Log Theater: 5175 Meadville.
130. Minnewashta School: 26350 Smithtown Road.

13

Gunflint Trail

The wilderness beauty of the area remains much as it was in the days of the voyageurs. Tall timber and numerous trails carpeted with centuries of pine needles invite the laughing footsteps of excited youngsters—and those who seek relaxing recreation.[1]

IN THE EARLY 1900s, U.S. government land surveyors explored the Gunflint Trail region of northern Minnesota, charting and naming its numerous lakes and streams. Jack Scott, a noted guide, hunter, and trapper, was hired to guide the party, and in the late fall, they reached the shores of what is now Hungry Jack Lake and set up a winter camp. When food sources dwindled, the surveyors snowshoed thirty-two miles into Grand Marais for provisions, leaving Scott behind to guard the camp.

The surveyors joined a holiday celebration in town but tarried too long. A devastating blizzard struck the north country, and it was two weeks before they could return to camp. Jack, nearly starved, heard them approaching and raced from the crude shack to meet them. "Hey, are you hungry, Jack?" one surveyor shouted. "Am I hungry, Jack!" Scott replied. "I'm nearly starved to death!" From that day on, the lake was named Hungry Jack.

In August 1942, Sinclair Lewis was living in Excelsior and was hard at work on *Gideon Planish*.[2] He had few friends in the Lake Minnetonka community, and he was searching for a winter home in the city. On August 5, his work was interrupted by the arrival of his son Michael, who had come to Minneapolis to visit.

Lewis planned to take his son on a camping trip in northern Minnesota, and another youngster, David Shiras, was asked to accompany them. As they rode northward, Lewis and his chauffeur, Joseph Hardrick, were soon worn out by the youngsters' incessant conversation. Young Shiras continually annoyed them with questions: When

120

would they arrive at Gateway? Would they like it? Would there be fish? Would the guide be white or Indian? What time would supper be served and would it be edible?

Michael Lewis, one year older and much taller than David, was too proud to ask questions. He posed as a know-it-all, narrating stories of how Indians had blazed trails or how tiresome it had become to see so many Coca-Cola signs along the highway.

Gateway-Hungry Jack Lodge was an ideal place to bring a boy, a wilderness paradise where a youngster could learn to appreciate the great outdoors. Sinclair Lewis was not the only personage to relax at the resort; the Weyerhaeusers, Congdons, Mayos, and other prominent Minnesota families came as well.[3] The original lodge, a rustic log cabin, had been erected in 1924 by Jesse Gapen.[4] In 1931 the lodge was destroyed by fire, but forty men and a foreman were hired through the winter of 1931–32 to cut down the huge white pine trees from the shores of Hungry Jack Lake and to float the logs to the lodge sites, where the timber was pulled from the lake by a team of horses. This structure, which opened in the summer of 1932, was the lodge that Sinclair Lewis came to know; it was the largest log structure in the Midwest, measuring 126 feet by 64 feet.

Lewis, Michael, David, and Joseph arrived at the lodge August 9.[5]

Gateway-Hungry Jack Lodge, Gunflint Trail in Northern Minnesota. Sinclair Lewis visited here in both 1942 and 1944 and wrote one of his better short stories, "All Wives are Angels" here. Photograph courtesy Gateway-Hungry Jack Lodge.

The author had rented two cottages for a week, one for the boys and Joseph, and a smaller one for himself. Lewis hoped to write.

In the afternoons, Lewis would drop in on the Jesse Gapens for long afternoon conversations with Mrs. Gapen.[6] She found the conversations stimulating and appealing but often disagreed with his criticisms of small-town residents. Lewis found the discussions equally rewarding, since Mrs. Gapen had grown up in a small Midwestern community and was familiar with small-town America. It had been twenty-two years since the publication of *Main Street*, but Lewis still defended his treatise, maintaining that small-town businessmen were cliquish and old-fashioned; he continued to attack their ideals and institutions. Mrs. Gapen insisted that small towns were places of wonder, delightful environments in which to grow up.

At fifty-nine, Lewis realized that his writing days were nearly over. The great books (*Babbitt* and *Main Street*) would never again be repeated, but he considered himself capable of writing a few more good ones. Ideas, like his books, were slow in coming; he continued to harp on the subjects that had brought him fame and hoped to rekindle the fire of his rebellious youth. But he now exhibited less energy and more room for compromise.

The Gapens quickly realized that Lewis was fond of the wilderness. He relished its beauty, its solitude, and the sagas of men like Jack Scott and Captain Billy Fawcett. The rustic cabins, constructed from towering white pines, appealed to him: This was the life the Minnesota pioneers had lived. Lewis made the best of the week and settled down to serious writing.[7] He had planned to work on the still incomplete *Gideon Planish* but did not touch the piece. Instead he wrote "All Wives Are Angels," the first of a series of short stories that took an offensive attitude toward women, for *Cosmopolitan*. He completed the story just before the end of the week and returned to Excelsior, where he hoped to tidy up *Gideon Planish*.

On July 22, 1944, Lewis, who then lived in Duluth, returned to Gateway-Hungry Jack Lodge with Marcella Powers, her mother, and Lewis's chauffeur, Asa Lyons.[8] They enjoyed Hungry Jack, and the author extended their stay through July 25, skipping a dinner party given by Margaret Culkin Banning in Duluth.[9] This marked Lewis's final visit to Hungry Jack Lake.

SINCLAIR LEWIS°SITE ON THE GUNFLINT TRAIL

131. Gateway-Hungry Jack Lodge: Thirty miles up the Gunflint Trail, 2½ miles from road to lodge.

14

Duluth

Superior Street now seems meagre, ill-constructed and assorted; a small town—the First National Bank's proud building just a huddle of assorted brick boxes.[1]

IN FEBRUARY 1944, Sinclair Lewis approached Margaret Culkin Banning at her Chatham Hotel suite in New York and demanded information about Duluth as well as a helping of ice cream.[2] Lewis subsequently invited Margaret to his own apartment; in the company of writer Henry Canby, old friend Deems Taylor, and Marcella and Mrs. Powers, he produced maps of the Duluth area. Lewis informed his guest that he planned to move to her city soon. Margaret responded quickly: She telephoned Kenneth Cant, a Duluth real estate agent, and asked him to locate accommodations for the author.

Lewis had been fond of Duluth since his introduction to the city during a visit to writer Claude Washburn in 1916.[3] He had written his early novel, *The Job*, in Duluth and later found the environment ideal for the completion of *Cass Timberlane*.

In a letter to Virginia Lewis dated March 31, 1944, he declared:

> After my lecture trip and writing a two part story for Cosmopolitan, I settled blissfully down to doing nothing but much reading. In a month or so I go out to Minnesota, and start my new novel after I get settled there for the summer.
>
> The chances are that I'll stay in Duluth—lack of gasoline makes the country too difficult, and Duluth will be so much cooler than any other city. I think I'll be able to get up along the North Shore by bus. I love that scenery up there, and would love to see more of it.

On May 17, 1944, the author arrived at the Hotel Duluth and immediately began searching for a house with Kenneth Cant.[4] Finally Lewis rented the spacious John G. Williams house, at 2601 East

Second Street, for the remainder of the year.[5] The elegant mansion boasted hand-crafted furniture by Hayden of New York, plush carpeting imported from Austria, five master bedrooms (two with fireplaces), two smaller bedrooms, a ballroom on the third floor, and a bowling alley in the basement. On January 1, 1945, Lewis purchased the house for fifteen thousand dollars, one-tenth its original price.

Lewis took his new novel seriously and abstained from liquor during his Duluth sojourn.[6] On the front patio, a favorite sitting place, he often compiled notes and wrote.[7] Fearing that the postman might deliver a greeting in addition to his mail and break his train of thought, he ordered the front steps walled up and left the sole entrance to the house in the rear.

Once settled, Lewis met Judge Mark Nolan, and the two became fast friends.[8] Nolan proved to be a valuable source for characterizations for *Cass Timberlane*, and the writer was present in court every morning at 10:00 A.M. After hiring taxi owner Asa Lyons as his chauffeur, Lewis followed Nolan about the circuit, and he quickly gained knowledge of judicial procedures.

Sinclair Lewis home, 2601 East 2nd Street, Duluth, Minnesota. Lewis rented this elegant house in May 1944 and subsequently purchased it on January 1, 1945. He remained here through 1946 and worked on two novels, Cass Timberlane and Kingsblood Royal here. Photograph by Eric Carlson, 1979.

"Cass Timberlane" house, Arthyde, Minnesota. This house was superimposed on Duluth and used as the setting for Lewis' novel, Cass Timberlane. Lewis visited here in 1944. Photograph by Eric Carlson, 1979.

Lewis finally discovered the prototype for Grand Republic, the setting for *Cass Timberlane*, in the tiny village of Arthyde.[9] "Buttermilk Alley," the road into Arthyde, was often washed out by rain, and the swampy terrain quickly provided a natural reservoir.[10] When Lewis stumbled upon it, the town consisted of a post office, Emmer's Store, the Arthyde Community Club (located in the town hall), and a Soo Line box car that served as a depot.[11] At the edge of town, Lewis chanced upon a house constructed entirely of stone; he announced to Lyons that here was Cass Timberlane's house.[12] Lewis superimposed Arthyde upon Duluth and produced his fictional metropolis, Grand Republic.[13]

Mark Nolan and Lewis also found camaraderie via the chessboard.[14] He frequently would invite Elsa Anneke and Jean Peyton to accompany the judge to the grueling chess matches so the women could keep Mrs. Powers company with Monopoly. This was no simple task, since Lewis owned a large white cat and poor Elsa was allergic to felines. During one of these sessions, when Mrs. Powers was out of the room, Peyton, observing a sniffling, wheezing, teary-eyed Anneke, proclaimed, "Elsa, don't we get into the damndest situations." The women were genuinely flattered to be asked along, but that fascination lasted only until they realized they were being used.

In Herbert and Ruth Dancer, Lewis found amity everlasting. Dancer served as Lewis's Duluth attorney, and he was very popular with the elite of Duluth society. Lewis liked him immediately and studied him for legal material that might be applied to *Cass Timberlane*. He experienced an even closer affinity for Mrs. Dancer, who wrote excellent poetry, which Lewis, for reasons unknown, declined to read.[15] The Dancers hosted lavish parties and invited the author of *Main Street*. At these receptions Lewis was introduced to the "right" people.

Other close acquaintances of the author included Pastor and Mrs. John Malick of the Unitarian Church, both of whom spent a great deal of time in the Lewis home.[16] The Malicks were active in the Little Theater of Duluth, and Lewis quickly showed interest in their acting endeavors.

In May 1944, Margaret Banning hosted a dinner party for Lewis at the local country club.[17] Shortly thereafter, Lewis reciprocated by inviting her to dinner. During the meal, he confessed to her that he hoped to marry Marcella Powers. She had served as his model for Jinny Marshland in *Cass Timberlane* but was young and had impressed no one in Duluth society as a suitable marriage partner for the great author.

Herbert Dancer house, 3131 East 1st St., Duluth. Dancer was Sinclair's Duluth attorney and his wife wrote excellent poetry. Photograph Eric Carlson, 1979.

Margaret Banning, meanwhile, was courted by wealthy Oliver Mining Company owner LeRoy Salsich. Salsich was a close friend of Lewis's and often entertained him at the Kitchi Gammi Club, located at 831 East Superior Street. It came as no surprise to Lewis that Margaret Banning and Salsich were married later in 1944.

During the summer of 1944, Lewis was visited by Minnesota painter, Adolph Dehn, whom he had met in New York. Describing himself, Dehn declared: "He is fond of Minnesota, especially in its tawny, subtle aspects in spring and autumn, but he is not yet the all-out professional Minnesotan Sinclair Lewis has become, nor can he rattle off from memory as Lewis can all the counties and county seats of the state."[18]

When Marcella and her mother came to Duluth, Margaret Banning gave a cocktail party for them.[19] It was at this party that Lewis met Robert and Kathy Ridder; he had met Robert's parents, the Victor Ridders, through Dorothy Thompson in New York. The Ridder family had founded a German newspaper in New York and pocketed a fortune by acquiring the *Long Island Daily News, New York Journal of Commerce, St. Paul Dispatch and Pioneer Press, Duluth Herald and News-*

Margaret Culkin Banning house, 617 Irving Place, Duluth. The well-known novelist lived here until her marriage to LeRoy Salsich in 1944. Photograph by Eric Carlson, 1979.

LeRoy Salsich home, 60 East Kent Road, Duluth. Wealthy Oliver Mining Company owner Salsich was a friend of Sinclair's and often entertained him at his club. Photograph by Eric Carlson, 1979.

Tribune; newspapers in Aberdeen, South Dakota, and Grand Forks, North Dakota; a minority interest in the *Seattle Times*; and half ownership of WTCN radio in Minneapolis.

Because of the war, there were few young couples in Duluth in 1944. Ridder's son, Robert, had been classified 4-F but held a commission in the U.S. Coast Guard and was stationed in Duluth. Though half a world away from the European and Pacific theaters, many Duluthians boasted, "We won the war in Duluth as we lost no battles there."[20] Lewis, then fifty-nine, took a shine to the young Ridders, even though they were half his age. He found them good listeners and a marvelous sounding board for whatever he wished to talk about. Robert worshipped Lewis, and the young couple often dined and went to parties with him. The Ridders always would pick him up at his quarters, a house they described as "cold, cavernous and empty." They, like others, were aware of the researching author's personality studies. But they weren't turned off by being used, even though they knew he was doing it.

Lewis habitually wore salt and pepper suits. After a party, the Ridders would drive their hero home and listen to him tear apart guests at the party, not in a malicious vein but in an amusing manner characterized by impressions and mimicry. Perceptive and reflective, Lewis missed nothing.

Lewis fussed with some local plays at the Little Theater and assisted with some of the productions through his association with the Malicks. On the opening night, when the Ridders took him home, he tore the play to pieces in the way he had mimicked the party people.

In July, Kathy Ridder was pregnant, and the couple vacated their tiny house on Superior Street and took lodgings with the Victor Ridders until the new house they had purchased was available for occupancy. Lewis came to the house daily and would play a round of chess with Robert. The author's appearance was unpleasant, and he required two shaking hands to lift his coffee cup to his mouth. The younger man was a poor chess player, and Lewis found great delight in punishing him, although Ridder did win a couple of matches.

With Marcella and her mother in town, Lewis was eager to introduce them to the Ridders. They came to tea July 30, 1944, but Kathy was in the hospital, having given birth to her first child two days before. After tea, Lewis longed to play chess, but Robert, his parents, and Kathy's mother wanted to visit Kathy in the hospital. Robert explained to Lewis that he would soon have to go, excited as he was over the new arrival. Nothing seemed out of the ordinary when Lewis and the Powers departed with the usual goodbyes.

A short time later, however, Lewis telephoned and berated Robert's mother for neglecting to fuss over Marcella and her mother. Mrs. Ridder was in a state of near shock when the angry author bellowed, "Your behavior was outrageous, and it has been an insult to both Marcella and her mother. Isn't that typical of conservative people?"

Astounded, she hung up, rejoined the family, and exclaimed, "You won't believe what we just had on the telephone." Thus ended the evening Lewis notes in his diary as "Last of the Ridders." Genuinely fond of Lewis, young Bob was injured the most. He would see the author at a party some time later, but the relationship would never be intimate again.

Lewis looked elsewhere for approval of Marcella. Accomplished musician Elsa Anneke had a daughter, Jean, about Marcella's age.[21] Lewis had, in fact, once asked Jean to marry him, but whether he was serious or not, he gave no indication. Elsa's good friend Jean Peyton, a gifted painter, also had a daughter Marcella's age. By inviting the Peytons and Annekes to parties, the scheming Lewis felt Marcella

Elsa Anneke in front of her home at 104 South 26th Avenue East in Duluth. Mrs. Anneke was one of the few loyal friends Lewis had when he left Duluth in 1946. Photograph by Eric Carlson.

would be included with people her own age and might easily be established as a member of the group.

Lewis often would drop by Elsa's house for conversation. One afternoon, Elsa issued a comment regarding Republicans. Lewis eyed her candidly and ejaculated, "I take it you and the people you are talking about are Republicans." Elsa replied in the affirmative. He remained quiet, and the conversation terminated. More often than not, a fiery Lewis would strike with verbal attacks on such political views, but this time he merely shortened his visit.

At parties, Marcella made a habit of sitting on the floor with her legs crossed in six-year-old fashion.[22] She seldom conversed with other guests, and most of Lewis's friends considered her just not with it. They ventured that she had no knowledge of literature, including that of Sinclair Lewis. No one in Duluth society understood his infatuation over someone they considered a silly youngster, especially after his having been married to such intellectual equals as Grace Hegger and Dorothy Thompson.

During one of Lewis's visits to Margaret Banning's summer retreat on the Brule River in northern Wisconsin, he again confided that he wished more than anything else to marry Marcella, but Margaret told him he was old enough to be Marcella's father, if not her grandfather.

On August 3, 1944, the Powers left Duluth, and Lewis followed them to New York August 28, escaping Minnesota's winter. In a letter to Virginia Lewis dated January 26, 1945, he related that he was still in New York, applying the finishing touches to *Cass Timberlane*:

> I've bought this delightful house I had in Duluth all last summer, and in mid-April I'm giving up this flat and moving out there with all my furniture. I doubt if I'll often spend more than six months a year there, because of the cold, but Duluth is enchanting in its cool summers, equally for work and for living. You'll probably be seeing the house before long.

He displayed concern for America, the war, and what would follow:

> It seems to me that though we civilians certainly have had no deprivations whatever, yet it may be said that America is coming through the war with amazing solidity. I'm afraid of racial feuds after the war, especially the gross childishness of anti-Semitism, but at least that attitude is no longer casually accepted and condoned by intelligent people—that's some gain.

He ended his letter with a splash of humor:

> Love, Jinny, and luck! My Duluth address will be 2601 East Second Street—which *sounds* like a piano warehouse.

In April 1945, Lewis and chauffeur Lyons returned to Duluth.[23] With no domestic servants available in Duluth, Lewis drove to Minneapolis to retrieve his faithful Lillian. While compiling data for his new book dealing with relations between whites and blacks (a volume which became *Kingsblood Royal*), Lewis pondered the question of equality. Frequently, when finished with the evening newspaper, he would walk into the kitchen and exclaim, "Lillian, here is the paper."[24] Lillian and Joseph, both of whom were black, would often be invited to dine with him and Mrs. Powers. He interviewed black leaders involved in the civil rights movement and made friends with members of the National Association for the Advancement of Colored People.[25] He gave parties that blended the cream of Duluth society with black leaders such as Edward Nichols, head of the NAACP, and Reverend Bert of the Methodist church.[26] He once even berated his white society guests for not inviting Negroes to their own parties. (In 1946 he went so far as to take a short leave from Duluth to visit the South so he could study the Negro and the white backlash.)

St. Mark's African Methodist Church, 502 E. 6th St., Duluth. Lewis frequently attended services here with his servants while doing research for *Kingsblood Royal*. Photograph by Eric Carlson.

He put more than black-white relations to the test. At one party, attended by Judge Nolan and the superintendent of schools, he invited both Catholic priests and Jewish rabbis.[27] He even planned a confrontation with his friend Father Cashen to convince the clergyman that there was no God.[28]

Lewis sometimes attended St. Mark's African Methodist Church with his servants.[29] On the day Japan surrendered, he handed Lillian and Mrs. Powers each a dollar while the three huddled in the church during the offering. Following the sermon, the preacher eyed the author and remarked, "We'd better pass the plate again."

Lewis frequently was invited to parties simply because he was a famous man.[30] More often than not, a personality clash occurred and he was not asked back. The author felt he was lionized by society people who were eager to show him off.[31] Guests regarded Lewis's own parties as dull, but the host found them far from tedious.[32] He once served a single bottle of scotch to a house full of guests.

While Margaret Banning was visiting friends in Minneapolis, Lewis telephoned her husband, LeRoy Salsich, asking him to arrange a party with all the right people; he had an important guest he wanted to impress. Salsich conveyed the message, and Margaret hosted the party at great expense. Everyone was in attendance, but Lewis failed to arrive until the final moments. He and his friend arrived, remained ten minutes, and departed. His hosts were understandably disconcerted.

Lewis gained a reputation for organizing parties, only to pop in and depart, or not to show up at all. Through this ruse he sought both attention and the creation of mystery.

Lewis's close friend Marvin Oreck, who supervised a department store, was married to an Australian actress.[33] During one of Lewis's afternoon teas, Mrs. Oreck flitted into the room and, admiring an original painting, clasped her hands and cried, "Oh, Sinclair, the southern coast of France." The painting had been done by a local artist, and Lewis, always talking in satire, replied, "Oh, Margot, the northern coast of Lake Superior."

Marvin Oreck house, 3501 East 2nd Street, Duluth. Oreck, who ran a popular department store, was a good friend of Lewis's during his Duluth sojourn. Photograph by Eric Carlson.

On another occasion, Lewis hosted a large party, inviting a couple hundred guests. One of his associates had a mistress, and no one ever invited the man's wife because he always brought his girlfriend. A cagey Sinclair Lewis invited both wife and mistress, and while the quarry squirmed, the author's typewriter clacked upstairs.

Lewis's parties always ended abruptly at 11 P.M. When the hour arrived, the monarch would proclaim, "For God's sake, aren't people ever going home?"

The author always was irritated when only he, and not Mrs. Powers, was invited to a social function. If Mrs. Powers was excluded, he would boycott the party. During the entire summer of 1945, he had altercations with nearly everyone with whom he associated in Duluth.[34]

A letter to Virginia Lewis dated July 26, 1945, suggests Lewis was a lonely man living in an empty house:

> I do hope that you will be able to keep your promise and return in fall, so that we shall be able to see you again. But it will probably be in NY that I shall see you, not here. I'm likely to leave for there in September, and come back here in early May, next year. I have brought all my furniture here from New York, and with some that I bought with the house, and a little new stuff, the house is in beautiful shape. It is a rather big place, very solidly built, but its greatest virtue is its situation. About 300 feet above the lake, with the ground in front of it dropping off sharply, it has a wonderful view of the lake and of the hills on the shore, or near it, to the East. I have done nothing much this summer but fuss with the house, and wander around here, and make plans for a novel which I shall not start writing till early next year.

The author's experiments were not limited to the super rich or the suffering downtrodden but included the breed of Babbittry he had written about in his native Sauk Centre. There were parties with Charlie Liscomb, Ken Cant, Lou Castle, Fred Buck, John Hoff, Arthur Miller, and Winton Brown—the influential bankers, insurance brokers and real estate men. Lewis even arranged a harbor tour by boat with these same individuals.[35] In July 1945, he attended a meeting of the Duluth Kiwanis Club and cited its officers—C. Elmer Hammer, Harry C. Applequist, Miss Dorothy Tart, and Jackson K. Ehlert—jesting only he could have made up such names.[36]

His next door neighbor, Evelyn Glendenning, and he formed a friendship.[37] After waving to each other daily, Mrs. Glendenning worked up enough nerve to bring him a piece of apple pie. Lewis grew to like her because he considered her anything but a "yes" person and described to her the article he was writing on assignment for *Esquire*. They met when Lewis accidently broke her fence, and they frequently chatted in what he termed his informal garden. To her, Lewis always referred graciously to his first wife, Grace, but never was complimentary of his second, Dorothy. "Living with Dorothy was like living in Grand Central Station," Lewis told Mrs. Glendenning. Yet, with other friends in Duluth he always spoke with respect for Dorothy.

During the course of a Monopoly game, Lewis bestowed upon his neighbor advice that would appear very chauvinistic by today's standards: He said women should never play chess, that it was a game for men like Oreck and Nolan. But he did add, "Never play a game, my dear, at least not with men, as only then does your calculating shrewdness show through." The relationship remained a platonic one, and Lewis displayed his appreciation for her by remarking: "You have causes but don't wave flags. You are curious but never inquisitive."

Once while he and Evelyn Glendenning were enjoying lunch at the Hotel Duluth, Valentine Saxby, executive secretary of the local chamber of commerce, approached them and proclaimed, "I saw the list of America's ten foremost writers in *Esquire*, and you were one of them. My God, Sinclair, where was Margaret [Banning]?" "Where the hell do you think she was?" bellowed Lewis. "She wasn't one of them." Attempting to calm the boisterous author, Mrs. Glendenning whispered, "After all, Mr. Lewis, Mrs. Banning had to write for money; she had four children to support." "Why the hell do you think anyone writes?" the unsympathetic Lewis snapped.

On October 29, 1945, Lewis's oldest son, Wells, was killed in the war.[38] He grieved over Wells' passing and would not talk about him for years to come. When John Gunther's book about the loss of his own son was published, Lewis was unable to understand how any father could write about such a tragedy.

Wells was not the only loss that year. Marcella Powers was seeing bandleader Michael Amrine in New York and consented to marry him.[39] Lewis was deeply hurt.

Despite his haggard appearance, Lewis was self-disciplined and meticulous.[40] He enjoyed daily walks and at disconcerting moments would produce a notebook from his back pocket and make notations. This habit of perpetual note taking was ritually carried out whether he was alone or with others.

He awoke every morning at 4:00 A.M. and wrote consistently until

8:00 A.M. During this period, he consumed numerous cups of coffee. Subsequently, he would arouse the household, and Lillian would prepare "a real Minnesota farm breakfast." He then either would write or would return to bed until lunch. He seldom did any writing in the afternoons, which he considered too noisy for serious work. It was then that he craved company and conversation.

Though scores of his friendships were strained, Lewis was besieged by visitors. Claude and Mary Lewis appeared that summer, and Harry rushed them to Elsa Anneke's door.[41] The visit came as a surprise: Elsa was forced to jump into a tattered red and gold negligee. Daughter Jean found sanctuary in a slightly better garment. As the staid and conventional Claude Lewises were introduced to them, Elsa felt like a "damn fool." The doctor from St. Cloud probably considered the women just more of his brother's crazy friends.

Budding writers Ann Chidester and Frederick Manfred called on the author in Duluth.[42] During tea, the host asked his guests to choose among three titles he had proposed for his new novel: Kingson, Kingsblood, or Kingsman.[43] Both of the writers chose *Kingsblood Royal* and Lewis agreed. Ann then nearly whipped Lewis at chess. (It must be remembered that it was always he who had boasted chess was strictly a man's game.) He wanted to talk about Minnesota as well as chess, and they discussed Midwestern authors. Lewis related that he was a member of the middle class, that there would always be a middle class, and that he would always write about it. Yet he confessed to a friend that he regretted in his own essential ways that he was so middle class.[44] Acquaintances were quick to recognize the dichotomy of his nature.

Son Michael visited his father that summer; so did author John Gunther, who was working on his book *Inside U.S.A.*[45] J. Harold Kittleson, a buyer from Random House in New York, arrived later.[46]

During the summer of 1945, Lewis gave the commencement address, entitled "The Excitement of Learning," at Duluth State Teachers College.[47] He also conducted a series of summer lectures called "The Craft of Writing," during which he delivered the following advice: "Writing is just goddamned hard work. It's ninety-nine percent hard work. The only way to write is to write. I work like hell when I write. I work as hard as anyone. Write! No one can teach you."[48] The students were disappointed, for they had expected to hear great wisdom dished out; none was forthcoming. Lewis, now sixty, failed to shock them as a younger Lewis would have done. He nonetheless possessed his old humor. During one lecture he apologized for his "new store teeth," which were responsible for his twangy speech, and he spoke about communism:

When I have a sympathetic communist in a book, all the reactionary reviewers say I'm pro-communist. That's what happened when I wrote "It Can't Happen Here." And then I wrote another with a no good communist character and all the communists jumped on me and said I was getting reactionary and anti-communist. I'm not pro-communist, but I'm not anti-communist either. Some communists are good people and some are no good.[49]

One woman in the audience, twenty-four-year-old Betty Alexander, had known the author at the University of Minnesota.[50] She had been employed by United Press in Chicago in 1943 and the *St. Louis Star-Times,* and had been active in the labor movement (Congress of Industrial Organizations) at the University of Minnesota. While she recuperated from a tonsillectomy and stayed with her aunts Lydia and Rose Bartholdi in Duluth, Lewis invited her out.

Betty's aunts were impressed with Lewis and excited over his having shown interest in Betty. They were overwhelmed by the big limousine that called for her, and they considered Lewis and Betty two of a kind, both offbeat. He tried teaching her chess but failed miserably. He still maintained chess was not a woman's game but was sympathetic to the women's movement in progress. Since women were men's equals, he felt they should carry their own cigarettes, and he was always relieved when Miss Alexander provided her own. He once remarked to her, "If there's anything I can't stand, it's people who bum cigarettes."

Returning from outings, Lewis, as usual, would mimic the people they had met, acting out the parts of ministers, politicians, and businessmen. He discussed with her the plot for his long-awaited labor novel (which he would never write): A radical organizer comes in to organize a factory. The daughter of the boss falls in love with him and a romance ensues. The father, a kind of Dodsworth character rather than an antiunionist, tells his workers they must join the union.[51]

Lewis had curiously ambivalent feelings about radicals. He resented their lack of humor and considered them conformists. Yet he admired their organization of mass protests. His stereotype of a communist centered upon those other people—foreign-born, not American, not middle class, and not tinged at all by any kind of agrarian radicalism. He theorized that Minnesotans who called themselves communists were merely good old-fashioned populists turned Farmer-Laborites. His sympathies remained with ordinary people, and he detested any type of pretense. When a popular left-wing writer was incarcerated, Lewis penned a letter in his behalf. When Henry Wallace campaigned for political office, Lewis quipped to Miss Alexander, "Then, sure, all the Meltons, the Howards, and the Irvings in New York will be supported." He always seemed too radical for the conservatives and too conservative for the radicals.

Once when the Glendenning children were playing noisily on the Lewis property, Evelyn called, "Should I send them home?"[52] He replied with much patience: "Oh, no, to children all property is communal. If they get rowdy, I'll send them home."

Lewis's socialistic tendencies were at best confined to paper. He worshipped Debs almost as a Christ figure, but he also campaigned for Harold Stassen. He attacked the rich for their lavish mansions and use of servants, but all of his own houses were monuments of pomposity, and he, too, employed servants and chauffeurs. He admired the Fabians in England but also referred to them as "parlor pinks." Regarding Fabians, he ventured, "If you offered them a hundred dollars, they'd be the first to take it and spend it on themselves." Above all, he was an astute reformer with no party affiliation. He deeply resented the rich gobbling the poor but embraced free enterprise as a way of life. When someone referred to the Iron Range as a mining camp, Lewis retorted, "What the hell do you call Duluth but a mining camp with merely overseers here? The lord of the manor is in New York City."

Twice he was invited to the Duluth home of liberal attorney, Henry Paull, and Mrs. Paull recalls in a letter:

> I can't understand how such a democratic man was so attracted to such people and why he sought them out. He ended up by insulting them and making enemies of them. As to the people he met at my house . . . I felt they were merely proletarian window dressing or something. He didn't seem interested in them as people or try to make friends among them. Yet, we would have been far more accepting, more compassionate than the people he chose to surround himself with. The man who wrote "Babbitt" actually loved Babbitts. The man who hated "men of measured merriment" chose men of measured merriment as companions. No wonder he was lonely.[53]

Conservative or radical, Sinclair Lewis suffered from a bad conscience regarding his keeping of servants.[54] He wished to treat his servants as equals and made a point of introducing them to everyone he knew. Once, after dropping off Betty Alexander, he jumped into the front seat with his chauffeur, Joseph. "I think it's foolish for two grown men to ride one in the front and one in the back," he said.

He expressed hope that *Kingsblood Royal* would change attitudes and bring about changes for blacks. Haunted by reviews, he discussed with Miss Alexander the critics' dissection of *Kingsblood*: A Minnesota banker discovers he has a tinge of black blood and brings it out in the open. One would certainly not go out and confess but would keep it a family secret, the critics said. He would never dig up the black ancestor and flaunt him before the townspeople. That was the last thing he would do. In his own defense, Lewis answered: "But what they didn't understand is that he was an honest man."

Just before his final departure from Duluth in 1946, Lewis telephoned Margaret Banning with a proposal: He wanted to trade houses.[55] Margaret lived in a fashionable mansion on Kent Road; she had never liked the Lewis house and considered it ugly. Lewis insisted on the house exchange, but Margaret stood her ground.

In January 1946, he sold his Duluth house for twenty thousand dollars but stayed on into March as a tenant.[56] Sad, lonely, and dejected, he referred to Duluth as "Margaret Banning's town," never his, and he counted his only friends as Judge Nolan, Marvin Oreck, Mrs. Malick, and the ever-faithful Asa Lyons. Nonetheless, Elsa Anneke, Jean Peyton, and the Dancers all came over to see him off.[57] His search for inner peace would lead him elsewhere; he felt he had little reason for staying.[58]

He considered himself a has-been. Sixty years old, he maintained no close relationships with anyone. Neither of his marriages had lasted, his eldest son was dead, and the young woman of a longstanding friendship had married someone else. There he was, rattling around a big, empty house with black servants. What a life for a Minnesota rebel who had intended to make the world better.

Mrs. Paull describes the aging author's haggard appearance and loneliness:

> When he appeared at the door I was taken aback, absolutely shocked. There stood a man so tall and thin he looked one-dimensional. No color in his face . . . a kind of graveyard grey. He looked as if he had been buried a month and been dug up.
>
> As the evening wore on, color seemed to appear in his face. . . . He began to look more human and more like a living man. I began to feel an enormous compassion for him as he seemed like the loneliest man I had ever met. He sat beside me on the couch and clung to my hand, and when-

Thorvale Farm, Williamstown, Massachusetts in 1947. Lewis lived here from 1946 to 1949. Photograph courtesy Isabel Lewis Agrell and Virginia Lewis.

> ever I got up to go into the kitchen or do some hostess job somewhere, he would be waiting with outstretched hand when I returned. This was not because he was attracted to me in any way. He was simply lonely and had to cling to somebody. I sensed a strange fear in him, fear of being deserted by mankind.[59]

Perhaps Betty Alexander said it best:

> I was sure he'd be East, too, because he had come home to find his roots, but he had found no soil to nourish them. The red and black earth of his own land is rich enough to have nourished him, and it should have, but it didn't. The love and labor of his own people should have welcomed him home but they didn't. Why he, like his friend Thomas Wolfe, found that he couldn't go home again, is a thing to wonder about. When he returned to stay, it was to be buried in Sauk Centre, after he died alone in Italy in 1951.[60]

SINCLAIR LEWIS SITES IN DULUTH

132. Herbert Dancer residence: 3131 East First Street.
133. Jean Peyton residence: 1605 East Second Street.

134. Kenneth Cant residence: 1617 East Second Street.
135. Victor Ridder residence: 2216 East Second Street.
136. Sinclair Lewis residence: 2601 East Second Street.
137. Evelyn Glendenning residence: 2621 East Second Street.
138. Judge Mark Nolan residence: 2125 East Third Street.
139. Asa Lyons residence: 1711 East Sixth Street.
140. Bartholdi residence (Betty Alexander): 1915 East Seventh Street.
141. Margaret Culkin Banning residence: 617 Irving Place.
142. LeRoy Salsich residence: 60 East Kent Road.
143. Elsa Anneke residence: 104 South Twenty-sixth Avenue East.
144. Claude Washburn residence: 101 Oxford (razed).
145. Robert Ridder residence: 2615 East Superior Street.
146. Kitchi Gammi Club: 831 East Superior Street.
147. Marvin Oreck residence: 3501 East Second Street.
148. Reverend Malick residence: Holland Hotel.
149. Hotel Duluth (Sinclair Lewis): 231 East Superior Street.
150. Charles Liscomb residence: 2532 East Fourth Street.
151. Lewis G. Castle residence: 2600 Greysolon Road.
152. Fred Buck residence: 2231 East Second Street.

Mark Nolan home: 2125-3rd St. East, Duluth. Photograph courtesy Eric Carlson, 1981.

153. John Hoff residence: 2417 East Third Street.
154. Winton Brown residence: 2323 East Third Street.
155. Arthur Miller residence: 411 Lake View Avenue.
156. St. Mark's African Methodist Church: 502 East Sixth Street.
157. Henry Paull residence: 4716 London Road.
158. John B. McConaughy residence: 304 North Thirteenth Street.
159. Edward Nichols: 1230 North Seventh Avenue East.

SINCLAIR LEWIS SITE IN ARTHYDE

160. "Cass Timberlane" house: Richard Anderson residence.

Notes

FOREWORD

[1] John Corry, "'Main Street' Caught up in Main Stream," *Minneapolis Star*, February 10, 1966.

[2] Meridel LeSueur, interview with author September 26, 1979.

[3] Donald Wandrei and Clement Haulpers, interviews with author.

[4] John T. Flanagan, "The Minnesota Backgrounds of Sinclair Lewis' Fiction," *Minnesota History*, 37 (1960): 1–13.

[5] "Red Lewis Discovers Minnesota," *Minneapolis Tribune*, June 2, 1942.

[6] (New York: Random House, 1949), p. 422.

CHAPTER ONE

[1] Sinclair Lewis, *Main Street* (New York: Harcourt, Brace & World, 1920), pp. 26–27.

[2] Ben DuBois, *A Historical Sketch of Sauk Centre* (Sauk Centre: First State Bank of Sauk Centre, 1954), pp. 8–12.

[3] *Ibid.*, pp. 12–13.

[4] *Ibid.*, p. 16.

[5] E. L. Kells, letter to author dated August 18, 1979.

[6] Mark Schorer, *Sinclair Lewis: An American Life* (New York: McGraw-Hill Book Co., 1961), p. 6.

[7] *Ibid.*, p. 21.

[8] Isabel Lewis Agrell, interview with author September 9, 1979.

[9] Schorer, p. 16.

[10] *Ibid.*, pp. 16–17; Agrell interview.

[11] Ben and Pat DuBois, interview with author July 14, 1979.

[12] Mrs. Charles McCadden, undated letter (August 1979) to author.

[13] Memoirs of Juliette Gates Moulton recorded in a letter by Mrs. George Eldridge to author dated November 1, 1979.

[14] Schorer, pp. 22, 30, 40–41.

[15] Schorer, p. 34.

[16] *Ibid.*, p. 64.

[17] Palmer House brochure.

[18] Schorer, pp. 33–34.

[19] Eleanor Ostman, "Palmer House Lease on Life Is Rejuvenated," *St. Paul Pioneer Press*, August 5, 1979.

[20] Schorer, p. 34.

[21] Ben and Pat DuBois interview.

[22] Grace Hegger Lewis, *With Love from Gracie* (New York: Harcourt, Brace & Co., 1955), pp. 88–89.

[23] William McCadden, interview with author November 18, 1979.

[24] John Brownell, *Milwaukee Journal*, April 30, 1979.

143

[25] Kells, letter to author dated November 23, 1979. Letter from Katherine DuBois to Kells.

[26] Kells, letter to author dated August 8, 1979.

[27] Ben and Pat DuBois interview.

[28] Sinclair Lewis, "The Long Arm of a Small Town," *Sauk Centre Annual*, 1931.

[29] Barnaby Conrad, "A Portrait of Sinclair Lewis: America's Angry Man in the Autumn of His Life," *Horizon*, March 1979, p. 48.

[30] Lewis, "Small Town."

[31] Schorer, p. 313.

[32] Agrell, letter to author dated November 5, 1979.

[33] Schorer, pp. 404–5.

[34] Ben and Pat DuBois interview.

[35] Schorer, pp. 461–63.

[36] *Ibid.*, pp. 502–3.

[37] *Ibid.*, p. 427.

[38] *Ibid.*, p. 599.

[39] *Ibid.*, p. 686.

[40] *Ibid.*, p. 743.

[41] *Ibid.*, p. 765.

[42] Agrell interview.

[43] C. Rathe, "On the Occasion of Sinclair Lewis' Burial," *South Dakota Review* 7 (Winter 1969–70): 44.

[44] Glanville Smith, letter to author dated December 31, 1979.

[45] Agrell and Frederick Manfred, interviews with author. Some biographers have stated that as the urn was lowered a gray, puffy cloud floated gently back toward Sauk Centre. Manfred says that the frigid twenty-six below zero temperature was responsible for the vapor that formed but that there was no puffy cloud and that it certainly did not float back toward Sauk Centre.

CHAPTER TWO

[1] Peter Brand, "A Letter from Sauk Centre," *Carleton Miscellany* I(2): 103.

[2] Edward L. Henry, *Micropolis in Transition* (Collegeville, Minn.: Center for the Study of Local Government, St. John's University, 1971).

[3] Isabel Lewis Agrell, interview with author September 9, 1979; and Virginia Lewis, interview with author July 28, 1980.

[4] Agrell letter to author dated October 1, 1979.

[5] Dr. Ochsner is referred to frequently in Helen Clapesattle, *The Doctors Mayo* (Minneapolis: University of Minnesota Press, 1941).

[6] Mark Schorer, *Sinclair Lewis: An American Life* (New York: McGraw-Hill Book Co., 1961), pp. 139–40.

[7] Dr. Charles F. Brigham, Jr., interview with author December 15, 1979.

[8] Brigham, letter to author dated December 1, 1979.

[9] Agrell interview.

[10] Grace Hegger Lewis, *With Love from Gracie* (New York: Harcourt, Brace & Co., 1955), pp. 96–97.

[11] Brigham interview.

[12] Glanville Smith, letter to author dated December 31, 1979.

[13] Agrell interview; Schorer, p. 336.

[14] Mrs. Ralph H. Rosenberger, undated letter (November 1979) to author.

[15] Smith letter.

[16] Rosenberger letter

[17] Brigham interview.

[18] Dr. Harry B. Clark, letter to author dated November 23, 1979.

[19] St. Cloud city directories.

[20] Virginia Lewis interview.

[21] Brigham interview.

[22] Agrell interview.

[23] Schorer, p. 599.

[24] Brigham interview.

[25] Brigham letter.

[26] Smith letter.

[27] Virginia Lewis interview.

CHAPTER THREE

[1] Mark Schorer, *Sinclair Lewis: An American Life* (New York: McGraw-Hill Book Co., 1961), p. 248. Letter from Sinclair Lewis to Mrs. Upton Sinclair (November 1917).

[2] *Ibid.*, p. 39.

[3] *Ibid.*, p. 65.

[4] Lucy Fricke, "Historic Ramsey Hill: Yesterday, Today, Tomorrow" (a pamphlet).

[5] Schorer, p. 248.

[6] Grace Hegger Lewis, *With Love from Gracie* (New York: Harcourt, Brace and Co., 1955), pp. 113–15.

[7] Theodore C. Blegen, *Minnesota: A History of the State* (Minneapolis: University of Minnesota Press, 1963), pp. 300–302.

[8] Grace Hegger Lewis, p. 115.

[9] January 18, 1918.

[10] Grace Hegger Lewis, p. 116.

[11] John J. Koblas, *F. Scott Fitzgerald in Minnesota* (St. Paul: Minnesota Historical Society Press, 1978), pp. 40–41.

[12] Evelyn Glendenning, interview with author September 8, 1979; Margaret Culkin Banning, interview with author July 22, 1979.

[13] Glendenning interview.

[14] Meridel LeSueur, interview with author September 26, 1979.

[15] Harold E. Stassen, letter to author dated October 6, 1980.

[16] Ben and Pat DuBois, interview with author July 14, 1979.

[17] Schorer, p. 644.

[18] *Ibid.*, pp. 693–701.

[19] Stassen letter.

[20] Schorer, pp. 686–93.

[21] Lucile Kane, telephone conversation with author July 25, 1979.

[22] Frederick F. Manfred, "Sinclair Lewis: A Portrait," *American Scholar* 23 (spring 1954): 184.

[23] Schorer, pp. 766–67.

[24] Betty Stevens, "A Village Radical: His Last American Home," *Venture* 2 (autumn 1956): 37.

CHAPTER FOUR

[1] Unpublished ballad of Sinclair Lewis given to author by Mrs. Joseph Herman, Cass Lake.

[2] Mark Schorer, *Sinclair Lewis: An American Life* (New York: McGraw-Hill Book Co., 1961), p. 250.

[3] Grace Hegger Lewis, *With Love from Gracie* (New York: Harcourt, Brace & Co., 1955), p. 116.

[4] Letter from Stanley A. Johnson, director of the Cass County Historical Society, to author dated November 17, 1980.

[5] Grant Utley, letter to author dated June 23, 1979.

[6] Theodore C. Blegen, *Minnesota: A History of the State* (Minneapolis: University of Minnesota Press, 1963), pp. 330–36.

[7] *Ibid.*

CHAPTER FIVE

[1] "Minnesota Diary of Sinclair Lewis" reprinted in Mark Schorer, *Sinclair Lewis: An American Life* (New York: McGraw-Hill Book Co., 1961), p. 685.

[2] *Ibid.*, pp. 99, 140–42.

[3] *Ibid.*, pp. 252–55.

[4] Grace Hegger Lewis, *With Love from Gracie* (New York: Harcourt, Brace & Co., 1955), p. 122.

[5] Schorer, p. 665.

[6] *Ibid.*, pp. 684–90.

[7] Russell Roth, "The Return of the Laureate: Sinclair Lewis in 1942," *South Dakota Review* 7 (winter 1969–70): 3–10.

[8] *Ibid.*, p. 3.

[9] *Ibid.*, p. 5.

[10] Virginia Lewis, interview with author July 28, 1980.

[11] Schorer, p. 692.

[12] Roth, interview with author August 31, 1979.

[13] *Ibid.*

[14] Roth, "Return of the Laureate," pp. 4–5.

[15] Roth interview.

[16] This same Max Shulman would go on to write famous comic novels, plays, and television shows, such as *Barefoot Boy with Cheek*, *The Tender Trap*, and *The Loves of Dobie Gillis*.

[17] Brenda Ueland, interview with author August 23, 1979; Mrs. John Dalrymple, interview with author September 7, 1979.

[18] Mary E. Staples, "As I Remember Sinclair Lewis," *South Dakota Review* 7 (winter 1969–70): 11.

[19] Ueland interview.

[20] Sinclair Lewis collection, Weyerhaeuser Library, Macalester College, St. Paul.

[21] Ueland interview.

[22] Dalrymple interview.

[23] Schorer, p. 695.

[24] Sinclair Lewis collection, Weyerhaeuser Library.

[25] Robert Agrell, interview with author September 9, 1979.

[26] Meridel LeSueur, interview with author September 26, 1979.

[27] Roth interview.

[28] Sinclair Lewis, "A Minnesota Diary," *Esquire*, October 1958.

CHAPTER SIX

[1] Harrison Smith, *From Main Street to Stockholm: Letters of Sinclair Lewis 1919–1930* (New York: Harcourt, Brace & Co., 1952), p. 5. Letter to Roland Holt, vice president of Henry Holt & Co.

[2] Jared How, interview with author and Dianne Goldstaub, September 16, 1981.

[3] John Wilhelm Schmitt, interview with Dr. Hjalmar O. Lokensgard. Dr. Lokensgard had intended to write an article on Lewis and publish it in 1969 to commemorate the fiftieth anniversary of Lewis's stay in Mankato. Never having published the material, he donated his research to the author in 1979.

[4] Letter from Marcia T. Schuster, director of the Blue Earth County Historical Society, to author dated November 18, 1980.

[5] Mrs. Cecil Girvin, interview with author December 1, 1979; Emma Wiecking, interview with author December 1, 1979; the late Mrs. Jared How, interview with author December 1, 1979; Mr. and Mrs. Charles Butler, interview with author June 28, 1980; Mrs. Cecil Snow, interview with Dianne Goldstaub July 22, 1980.

[6] Undated newspaper clipping sent to Lokensgard by Anna Wiecking and then given to author.

[7] Lokensgard research.

[8] *Mankato Daily Free Press*, June 12, 1919, letter by Bronson West.

[9] June 16, 1919.

[10] *Mankato Daily Review*, June 24, 1919.

[11] *Mankato Daily Review*, June 4, 1919.

[12] Grace Hegger Lewis, p. 124.

[13] Lokensgard research.

[14] Grace Hegger Lewis, pp. 124–25.

[15] Mrs. Jared How interview; Mrs. George Bohannon, letter to author dated January 12, 1980.

[16] Mr. and Mrs. Charles Butler interview.

[17] Girvin interview.

[18] Mrs. Lee Wood, interview with Lokensgard September 22, 1969.

[19] Thomas Edwards, interview with Lokensgard September 22, 1969.

[20] Emma Wiecking interview and letter to author dated November 7, 1979.

[21] Girvin interview and letter to author dated October 4, 1979.

[22] Margaret Schmitt Habein, "I Remember Mankato," *Mankato Free Press*, May 29, 1952.

[23] Lois Swain, undated letter to author June 1979.

[24] *Mankato Daily Review*, July 10, 1919.

[25] *Mankato Daily Review*, July 12, 1919.

[26] Arlene Schwartz, interviews with author May 1979 and July 29, 1979.

[27] Grace Hegger Lewis, p. 126.

[28] *Mankato Daily Review*, July 28, 1919.

[29] Lokensgard research.

[30] Copy of *Free Air* owned by Mr. and Mrs. Charles Butler, copied by Dianne Goldstaub of *Mankato Free Press* for author during interview.

[31] Ken E. Berg, "Free (for a while)," *Mankato Free Press*, October 5, 1979; and Marcia T. Schuster, letter to author dated October 4, 1979.

CHAPTER SEVEN

[1] Sinclair Lewis, "A Minnesota Diary," *Esquire*, October 1958.

[2] Kenneth L. Smith, letter to author dated November 17, 1979.

[3] Smith, letter to author dated December 25, 1979.

[4] Smith letter dated November 17, 1979.

[5] Smith letter dated December 25, 1979.

[6] *Mankato Daily Review*, July 10, 1919.

[7] Arlene Schwartz, interviews with author May 1979 and July 20, 1979, and letter to author dated June 22, 1979.

[8] Smith letter dated November 17, 1979.

[9] Schwartz, letter to author dated November 29, 1979.

[10] Schwartz interviews.

[11] Lewis, "A Minnesota Diary."

[12] Schwartz, letter to author dated July 17, 1979; Mrs. Adolph Dehn, interview with author July 29, 1979.

[13] John K. Sherman, *Minneapolis Tribune*, July 2, 1944.

[14] Dehn interview.

[15] Sherman, *Minneapolis Tribune*.

[16] *Ibid.*

CHAPTER EIGHT

[1] Sinclair Lewis, *Mantrap* (New York: Harcourt, Brace & Co., 1926), p. 8.

[2] Isabel Lewis Agrell, interview with author September 9, 1979.

[3] Diary of Claude Bernard Lewis in the possession of Agrell.

[4] Charles F. Brigham, Jr., interview with author December 15, 1979.

[5] Claude Lewis diary.

[6] Papers of Claude Lewis in possession of Agrell.
[7] Claude Lewis diary.
[8] Papers of Claude Lewis.
[9] Claude Lewis diary.
[10] Papers of Claude Lewis.
[11] Claude Lewis diary.
[12] Papers of Claude Lewis.
[13] Letter dated July 30, 1925.
[14] (Harcourt, Brace & Co., 1926), pp. 29–30.
[15] *Ibid.*, pp. 32–33.
[16] *Ibid.*, pp. 39–41.
[17] *Ibid.*, p. 69.
[18] *Ibid.*, p. 12.
[19] Brigham interview.

CHAPTER NINE
[1] Letter from Sinclair Lewis to Hugh Walpole reprinted in Mark Schorer, *Sinclair Lewis: An American Life* (New York: McGraw-Hill Book Co., 1961), p. 459.
[2] Breezy Point history provided by Lori Torbinson of Breezy Point Lodge during an interview September 1979; and David Gravdahl, interview with author September 9, 1979.
[3] Mr. and Mrs. Robert Hamilton, interview with author September 9, 1979.
[4] Schorer, pp. 448–55.
[5] Mr. and Mrs. Robert Hamilton interview.
[6] June 6, 1926.
[7] Schorer, pp. 459–60.
[8] Isabel Lewis Agrell, interview with author September 9, 1979.
[9] Virginia Lewis, interview with author July 28, 1980.
[10] Agrell interview.
[11] Schorer, p. 459.
[12] Agrell interview.
[13] James Ellwood, interview with author May 4, 1980.
[14] Agrell interview.
[15] Schorer, p. 459.

CHAPTER TEN
[1] Sinclair Lewis, conversation with Charles Breasted recorded in Mark Schorer, *Sin-*
[2] "Sinclair Lewis wrote 'Elmer Gantry' during Summer's Stay on Rain Lake," *International Falls Daily Journal*, January 11, 1951.
[3] Schorer, p. 461.
[4] Letter from Mary Hilke, executive secretary and curator of the Koochiching County Historical Society, to author dated July 30, 1979.
[5] "Sinclair Lewis," *International Falls Daily Journal*, January 11, 1951.
[6] Schorer, pp. 461–62.
[7] "Sinclair Lewis," *International Falls Daily Journal*, January 11, 1951.

CHAPTER ELEVEN
[1] Sinclair Lewis quoted in Mark Schorer, *Sinclair Lewis: An American Life* (New York: McGraw-Hill Book Co., 1961), p. 666.
[2] Schorer, pp. 662–65.
[3] Undated *Madison Capital Times* article mailed to author by Wayne J. Merbach of Madison.
[4] Schorer, pp. 665–66.

⁵ Prof. F. G. Cassidy, interview with R. Alain Everts January 29, 1981.

⁶ Schorer, pp. 665–66.

⁷ Cassidy interview.

⁸ Eleanor Wirig, interview with Everts February 1980.

⁹ Primrose Watters, interview with Everts January 31, 1981; Robert B. Doremus, interview with Everts February 6, 1981.

¹⁰ Mrs. Harry Hayden Clark, interview with Steven Lowe in 1972.

¹¹ Watters interview.

¹² Schorer, pp. 665–70.

¹³ Prof. Ricardo Quintana, interview with Everts February 5, 1981.

¹⁴ Doremus interview.

¹⁵ Clark interview.

¹⁶ Prof. Ellsworth Barnard, interview with Everts February 5, 1981.

¹⁷ Prof. Samuel Rogers, interview with Everts January 26, 1981.

¹⁸ Schorer, p. 667.

¹⁹ Gunnar Johansen, interview with Everts January 27, 1981.

²⁰ Margaret Waterman, interview with Everts February 5, 1981.

²¹ University of Wisconsin Directory for 1940–41. The *Wisconsin State Journal* for September 30, 1940, cites 222 Bascom Hall as the classroom Lewis used.

²² Mrs. Henry Pochman, interview with Everts January 31, 1981.

²³ Waterman interview.

²⁴ Letter from Sinclair Lewis to August Derleth dated February 9, 1938, from a collection at the Wisconsin State Historical Society, Madison.

²⁵ Letter in the Wisconsin State Historical Society collection.

²⁶ August Derleth, *One Hundred Books by August Derleth* (Sauk City, Wis.: Arkham House Publishers, 1962), pp. 32–48.

²⁷ Schorer, p. 669.

²⁸ Pochman interview.

²⁹ Cassidy interview.

³⁰ Barnard interview.

³¹ Waterman interview.

³² Pochman interview.

³³ Clark interview.

³⁴ Doremus interview.

³⁵ Johansen interview.

³⁶ Doremus interview.

³⁷ Doremus interview.

³⁸ Clark interview.

CHAPTER TWELVE

¹ Sinclair Lewis quoted in Mark Schorer, *Sinclair Lewis: An American Life* (New York: McGraw-Hill Book Co., 1961), p. 686.

² Mr. and Mrs. Rudolph Miller, interview with author August 10, 1979.

³ Alfred Clague, interviews with author August 6 and 7, 1979.

⁴ Mr. and Mrs. Rudolph Miller interview.

⁵ Theodore C. Blegen, *Minnesota: A History of the State* (Minneapolis: University of Minnesota Press, 1963), p. 201.

⁶ *Ibid.*, pp. 146–49.

⁷ Schorer, p. 687.

⁸ Virginia Lewis, interview with author July 28, 1980.

⁹ Schorer, p. 687.

¹⁰ Robert Aden, interview with author October 30, 1979.

¹¹ Leonard Garaghty, interviews with author July 30 and 31, 1979.

¹² Dr. Stuart Lane Arey, interview with author November 1, 1979.

¹³ Virginia Lewis interview.

CHAPTER THIRTEEN

[1] Gateway-Hungry Jack Lodge brochure.
[2] Mark Schorer, *Sinclair Lewis: An American Life* (New York: McGraw-Hill Book Co., 1961), pp. 688–89.
[3] Jerry C. Parson, undated letter (June 1979) to author.
[4] Lodge brochure.
[5] Schorer, pp. 688–89.
[6] Robert D. Gapen, letter to author dated July 16, 1979.
[7] Schorer, pp. 688–89.
[8] Engagement books of Sinclair Lewis, July 22–25, 1944, Beinecke Rare Book and Manuscript Library, Yale University.
[9] Schorer, p. 718.

CHAPTER FOURTEEN

[1] Sinclair Lewis, "A Minnesota Diary," *Esquire*, October 1958 (entry for March 11, 1946).
[2] Margaret Culkin Banning, interview with author July 22, 1979.
[3] Mark Schorer, *Sinclair Lewis: An American Life* (New York: McGraw-Hill Book Co., 1961), p. 235.
[4] *Ibid.*, p. 713.
[5] Mrs. Richard Spicer, letter to author dated July 20, 1979; Sister Paul Mary, interview June 1979.
[6] Robert Ridder, interview with author July 3, 1979; Elsa Anneke, interview with author July 21, 1979; Banning interview; Evelyn Glendenning, interview with author September 8, 1979.
[7] Sister Paul Mary interview.
[8] Banning interview.
[9] Schorer, p. 716.
[10] Richard Anderson, Edna Coolidge, Alice Modrow, and Carol Simonson, all interviewed by author July 21, 1979.
[11] In 1906 brothers Art and Clyde Hutchins and Guy Thompson each donated ten acres for a new town to be named after them (Art-Th-yde). Settled by Scotch-Irish immigrants, the town evolved from Charles Millward's Millward Township. Northrup's Store served as the original post office but became Walter Manula's Store prior to the arrival of Sinclair Lewis. Today the only remaining structure in Arthyde is the Richard Anderson house (Cass Timberlane house), and the town boasts a population of three.
[12] The house was built by a Mr. Sin in 1925 for $28,000. He died before he could take occupancy.
[13] Banning interview.
[14] Anneke interview and letter to author dated June 24, 1979.
[15] Banning interview.
[16] Anneke interview.
[17] Banning interview.
[18] John K. Sherman, *Minneapolis Tribune*, July 2, 1944.
[19] Robert Ridder interview July 3, 1979; and Kathy and Robert Ridder, interview with author October 10, 1979.
[20] Robert Ridder interview July 3, 1979.
[21] Anneke, letter to author dated August 17, 1979.
[22] Anneke, Banning interviews.
[23] Schorer, p. 729.
[24] Glendenning interview.
[25] Betty Alexander, interview with author October 14, 1979.
[26] Schorer, pp. 730–31.
[27] Glendenning interview.
[28] Anneke interview.

29 Glendenning interview.

30 Banning interview.

31 Alexander interview.

32 Banning interview.

33 Glendenning interview.

34 Anneke interview.

35 Schorer, p. 735.

36 Engagement books of Sinclair Lewis, July 1945, Beinecke Rare Book and Manuscript Library, Yale University.

37 Glendenning interview.

38 Alexander interview.

39 Banning interview.

40 Glendenning interview.

41 Anneke interview and letter.

42 Frederick Manfred, letter to author dated July 17, 1979.

43 Frederick F. Manfred, "Sinclair Lewis: A Portrait," *American Scholar* 23 (spring 1954): 162–84.

44 Alexander interview.

45 Schorer, pp. 735–36.

46 J. Harold Kittleson, interview with author August 15, 1979.

47 Schorer, p. 734.

48 Alexander interview.

49 Betty Stevens, "A Village Radical Goes Home," *Venture* 2 (summer 1956): 20.

50 Alexander interview.

51 According to Alexander, Lewis never wrote the novel because "it was a source of life, something he was not part of."

52 Glendenning interview.

53 Letter to author dated October 15, 1979.

54 Alexander interview.

55 Banning interview.

56 Schorer, pp. 743–45.

57 Anneke interview.

58 Alexander interview.

59 Paull letter.

60 Stevens, "A Village Radical Goes Home," p. 26.